The Buy Low Sell High Blueprint

A Proven System for Timing Markets, Mastering Cycles, and Building Real Wealth

Deepanshu Suman

2025 — First Edition

Copyright

Title: The Buy Low Sell High Blueprint
Author: Deepanshu Suman

First Edition
ISBN: 978-93-5525-846-5

Disclaimer: This book is for educational and informational purposes only. It explores principles of investing, market cycles, valuation, psychology, and decision-making. The content does not constitute financial, investment, legal, or professional advice. Readers should conduct their own research and, where appropriate, consult a qualified professional before making financial decisions based on this material.

Dedication

To everyone who chooses discipline over emotion,
clarity over noise,
and long-term wealth over short-term fear.

Acknowledgments

Writing this book has been a journey of clarity, discipline, and discovery—and it would not have been possible without the people who shaped my thinking and supported me along the way.

To the mentors, teachers, and thinkers who taught me to question assumptions, challenge noise, and study markets with patience and precision—your influence lives in every chapter of this book.

To the readers, learners, and curious minds who continue to seek better systems and better decisions—your pursuit of knowledge is the reason this work exists.

To my friends and family, thank you for your unwavering encouragement, for believing in my work even before I did, and for giving me the environment to think deeply and write honestly.

And finally, to everyone who has ever chosen to understand the cycle instead of reacting to it—this book is, in many ways, a reflection of your mindset. May it help you build both wisdom and wealth.

Preface

The financial world is filled with noise—opinions, predictions, headlines, and hype designed to pull investors from clarity into confusion. Yet, beneath that noise lies a single principle that has guided wealth creation for centuries: **buy low, sell high**.

Everyone knows it. Almost no one consistently practices it.

This book was written to close that gap.

I have seen how market cycles repeat, how fear blinds people during lows, and how euphoria traps them at highs. Over time, I learned that success in markets is less about forecasting and more about discipline—less about predicting the future and more about understanding human behavior.

The Buy Low Sell High Blueprint distills those lessons into a simple, repeatable framework. It is not a book of guesses, shortcuts, or secret formulas. It is a guide to thinking clearly, acting rationally, and aligning your decisions with the realities of cycles, value, and psychology.

My goal is not to impress you with complexity, but to empower you with clarity.

If this book does one thing for you—helps you avoid buying at the top or selling at the bottom—then it has already delivered its value many times over. But my hope is that it does more: that it gives you a lifelong framework for navigating markets with confidence and calm, no matter how chaotic the world becomes.

Thank you for choosing to read this.
Thank you for choosing to think differently.
And thank you for choosing wisdom over noise.

— *Deepanshu Suman*

The Rule Everyone Knows but Almost Nobody Follows

Overview

There is a single principle that quietly underpins nearly every great fortune ever made in markets:

Buy low. Sell high.

It is simple to state and fiendishly difficult to practice. This chapter explains why the rule fails in everyday life, sharpens what "low" and "high" actually mean, and shows how a repeatable system converts a platitude into persistent edge. By the end of this chapter you will understand the psychological, structural, and technical obstacles that prevent most people from following the rule — and you will have clear, practical tools to begin doing it correctly.

Why a Simple Rule Becomes Hard Practice

On paper the rule is trivial. In markets it is not. Five durable forces conspire to make a truth into a trap:

1. Emotion — the invisible trader

Markets are driven by human beings. Humans are emotional. Emotions are immediate and powerful: fear triggers selling to avoid loss; greed triggers buying to capture gains. These impulses are not small nudges. They dominate the decisions of retail investors and often influence professional behavior too.

Key biases and how they sabotage the rule:

- **Loss aversion:** Losing $100 feels worse than the pleasure of winning $100. This asymmetry pushes people to sell winners too early or hold losers too long.
- **Recency bias:** Recent returns shape expectations disproportionately. A long gain encourages more buying; a recent drop provokes panic selling.
- **Herding:** People assume the crowd knows something they do not. Herding creates momentum and euphoria that entice late buyers.
- **Confirmation bias:** Once invested, people seek information that confirms their choice and ignore opposing signals.

2. Lack of Valuation Knowledge — mistaking price action for value

Price is observed; *value* is estimated. Many investors see a price drop and call it "cheap" without testing whether the business or asset quality has permanently deteriorated. Conversely, rising prices are often accepted as validation rather than questioned for over-optimism.

Valuation need not be academic. A few robust, conservative checks can separate genuine bargains from value traps. Without those checks, "buy low" is merely wishful thinking.

3. No System — the tyranny of discretion

Without pre-defined rules, decisions become episodic and emotional. A system converts the principle into a process:

- Entry rules (what, when, and how much)
- Exit rules (targets and protection)
- Sizing rules (how big to make a bet)
- Review rules (how and when to reassess)

Systems reduce cognitive load and remove the need to "decide in the moment," which is exactly when people fail.

4. Market Noise — signal vs. static

Financial markets are noisy: headlines, analyst notes, macro forecasts, viral threads. Noise creates false alarms and false comforts. The core job is not to react to every signal but to separate transient noise from durable change. Systems and checklists help you filter noise consistently.

5. Human Wiring — biology versus markets

Our brains evolved for small-group survival, not for distributed, probabilistic markets. Evolution rewards social cohesion and short-term safety; markets reward contrarian thinking at extremes. That mismatch makes contrarian actions (buying in fear, selling in euphoria) psychologically costly.

Sharpening Terms: What Do "Low" and "High" Really Mean?

"Low" and "high" are not simply adjectives attached to price tags. They are states defined by the relation between price and value, and by the context driving price.

Low: the buying condition

An asset is in a **LOW zone** when the following *four* conditions are met:

1. **Price materially below a defensible value range.** Not a 1–2% whim, but a meaningful discount (common practical thresholds: 20–50%, depending on asset and conservatism).
2. **Fundamentals are intact or recoverable.** Revenue, cash flow, balance-sheet strength, or competitive position should not be permanently impaired.
3. **The decline is driven by temporary events or sentiment** (sector panic, macro scare, headline shock), not a permanent structural failure.
4. **Execution is feasible:** the market is sufficiently liquid that you can build your position without unduly moving price.

Insight: A low price alone is not a signal. Low price + durable business or asset + temporary cause = opportunity.

High: the selling condition

An asset is in a **HIGH zone** when the inverse pattern appears:

1. **Price exceeds a conservative fair-value range** by a substantial margin (often 30–100%+ depending on context).
2. **Narrative and emotion lead fundamentals.** Storytelling and expectations drive price more than underlying results.
3. **Parabolic, vertical moves are present.** Rapid price acceleration with retail mania signals fragility.

4. **Smart-money exit signs** (insider selling, institutions scaling down) are visible.

Insight: High price + narrative dominance + structural fragility = rational exit.

The Difference Between Knowing and Doing

Understanding these definitions is not enough. The critical gap is execution: converting knowledge into a reliable behavior pattern. That gap closes with a system — a documented, practiced method that handles the emotional, informational, and sizing challenges.

What a good system does

A good trading/investing system:

- Defines entry and exit conditions precisely.
- Sets sizing limits before the trade.
- Uses checklists to avoid impulsive deviations.
- Incorporates stress tests and post-mortems to learn.
- Is simple enough to be executed under pressure.

A Practical, Repeatable Framework — Preview

Later chapters expand this into templates and tools. Here is the high-level framework you will implement:

1. **Scan:** Screen for outsized moves and candidates (price swings, volatility spikes).
2. **Validate:** Quick fundamental triage: are core metrics intact?
3. **Value:** Produce a conservative fair-value range using simple methods (comparables, cash-flow back-of-envelope, multiples).
4. **Enter:** Buy in tranches when price trades inside the LOW zone with defined position sizing.
5. **Manage:** Monitor thesis, scale-in if conditions improve, protect downside with stops or hedges.
6. **Exit:** Execute scale-outs in the HIGH zone; use trailing protection on the remainder.

7. **Review:** Conduct a short post-mortem and codify lessons.

This is the BL-SH method in outline form. Each step is later explained with checklists and templates.

Deep Dives and Practical Examples

Practical learning is accelerated by concrete examples. Below are expanded scenarios showing the framework in action across different asset classes.

Case 1: A Quality Stock in Sector Panic (Equity)

Context: A leading consumer-packaged-goods company, *Company A*, reports a single bad quarter because of temporary supply disruptions in one region. The sector skids 35% as investors fear contagion.

Step-by-step analysis:

1. **Scan:** Price dropped 40% from 52-week highs.

2. **Validate fundamentals:** Company A still generates strong cash flow, has low net debt, and maintains brand strength. The supply disruption is local and fixable.

3. **Value:** Comparable multiples and a conservative DCF indicate fair value is only 20% below the prior price — current price presents a 40%+ buffer.

4. **Enter:** Initial tranche = 30% of intended full allocation. Document thesis and set a plan to add if price moves deeper or fundamentals improve.

5. **Manage:** Monitor inventory recovery and channel restocking; set an alert at 20% recovery and at 40% recovery to scale in.

6. **Exit:** If the market re-rates and price reaches 30–40% above conservative value (HIGH zone), sell 25–50

Result: Acting during fear, with a system and margin of safety, translated panic into a durable edge.

Case 2: A Crypto Token in Mania (Digital Asset)

Context: Token B doubles in three weeks after media hype. Social channels proliferate buy signals. New retail wallets flood the network.

Analysis:

1. **Scan:** Rapid parabolic move, volume surges, on-chain metrics show many new holders with low tenure.

2. **Validate fundamentals:** Protocol utility is real but monetization unclear; roadmap milestones are far off.

3. **Value:** Intrinsic valuation is speculative; use conservative multiples and on-chain indicators to set a high uncertainty discount.

4. **Enter / Exit:** For existing holders, follow a scale-out: sell 30–50

Result: Systematic profit-taking in euphoria avoids the classic pattern of being wiped out by a rapid retracement.

Case 3: Real Estate — Distressed Market Opportunity

Context: Local market sees prices drop 25% after interest-rate shock. A rental property with long-term cashflow and a fixed-rate mortgage becomes available at a discount.

Analysis:

1. **Scan:** Price down 25% relative to historical local market; tenants remain.

2. **Validate fundamentals:** Rental demand is steady; mortgage terms are favorable; cap rates remain attractive.

3. **Value:** Conservative cap-rate-based valuation shows a margin of safety versus replacement cost.

4. **Enter:** Use leverage prudently: initial down payment within risk limits, ensure cash buffer for higher rates, and plan for multi-year hold.

5. **Manage/Exit:** Hold for cashflow and wait for market normalization; consider partial sale or refinancing when local prices recover into the HIGH zone.

Result: Buying into a market panic with proper underwriting and a cash buffer produces superior long-term returns.

Tools You Can Use Immediately

Below are concrete checklists, rules, and templates you can apply right away. These are intentionally short so you will actually use them.

The LOW Checklist (Use first)

1. Is price $\geq$ 20% below my conservative fair value estimate?

2. Are core fundamentals intact (profitability, manageable leverage, market position)?

3. Is the decline mostly sentiment-driven or tied to a temporary event?
4. Can I build a meaningful position without moving the market?
5. Do I have a predefined maximum allocation for this idea?

If yes to most items, the asset qualifies as a LOW-zone candidate.

The HIGH Checklist (Use for exits)

1. Is price significantly above conservative fair value (30%+)?
2. Are narratives and headlines replacing fundamentals as the chief rationale?
3. Is price acceleration parabolic with high retail participation?
4. Are insiders or informed investors reducing positions?

If yes to two or more items, begin a structured scale-out and protect the balance.

Simple Position-Sizing Protocol

- **Max single idea allocation:** set a hard limit (e.g., 3–7% of portfolio).
- **Initial tranche:** 25–40% of the max allocation at first LOW-zone entry.
- **Add rule:** add only as price moves deeper into LOW or fundamentals improve; never exceed max allocation.
- **Take-profit rule:** sell 25–50% at predefined valuation milestones; use trailing stops on remainder.

Quick Valuation Recipes (practical, not academic)

1. **Comparable multiples:** use conservative peers' multiples (PE, EV/EBITDA) and apply a discount for uncertainty.
2. **Free-cash-flow proxy:** estimate stable cash flow and apply a 6–10% discount depending on risk to get a ballpark fair value.

3. **Replacement-cost check (real assets):** compare price to rebuild or replacement cost to ensure physical viability.
4. **Range approach:** always use a conservative (low) and bullish (high) fair value — trade within ranges, not single point estimates.

Common Objections and Practical Answers

"Markets can stay irrational longer than I can stay solvent."

Answer: Use strict sizing, staggered buying, and proper downside protection. Your system must preserve optionality.

"My valuation might be wrong."

Answer: Use conservative assumptions, prefer ranges, and require a margin of safety. If your thesis is highly uncertain, reduce size or treat the idea as speculation.

"Won't I miss rallies if I wait for lows?"

Answer: The framework allows tactical momentum entries (small size) but insists on converting to value-weighted positions once you have a margin of safety.

"How do I know when a decline is temporary vs. permanent?"

Answer: Focus on causal analysis. If the decline stems from macro fear, liquidity shock, or temporary business disruption, it is likely temporary. If it stems from structural market loss, technological obsolescence, or permanent loss of demand, it is likely permanent.

Mental Models to Internalize

These short, repeatable mental models build intuition:

- **Margin of Safety:** Buy with a buffer that cushions estimation error.
- **Optionality:** Smaller initial bets give you the option to add later if reality confirms your thesis.
- **Asymmetric Payoff:** Focus on situations where downside is limited and upside is meaningful.
- **Time Arbitrage:** Markets discount information quickly; you can exploit short-term fear to capture long-term returns.

Exercises (Practice Until It Becomes Habit)

1. **Post-Mortem:** Select a trade you lost money on or missed. Write a one-page analysis mapping which failure forces (emotion, valuation, system, noise, wiring) contributed.
2. **Three-Asset Checklists:** Apply the LOW and HIGH checklists to three assets you follow. Record answers and action decisions.
3. **Value Range:** For one asset, compute a conservative and bullish fair-value range using one of the quick recipes above.
4. **Sizing Plan:** Define your max allocation for an idea and create a three-tranche entry plan consistent with the position-sizing protocol.
5. **Behavioral Trigger:** Design one simple rule to prevent panic selling (e.g., never sell below 10% loss without a checklist review).

Summary: The Practical Takeaway

- **Knowing** the rule *buy low, sell high* is trivial; **doing** it requires systems, valuation, and psychological control.
- Define LOW and HIGH as relationships between price and defended value, moderated by fundamentals and sentiment context.
- Use a simple, repeatable framework (scan, validate, value, enter, manage, exit, review).
- Start small: use the checklists, apply conservative valuation, and practice the exercises.

Closing thought

A truthful rule becomes a competitive advantage when you design the mechanics to follow it. The rest of this book converts each component of the framework into a practical tool: valuation templates, cycle recognition charts, psychological guardrails, execution checklists, case studies, and a one-page master plan you can use for life. Begin with the checklists in this chapter. Practice them on three assets this week. The habit — not the idea — builds enduring advantage.

Contents

Chapter 1

The Law of Value: What Low Really Means

Introduction

Everyone repeats the idea of "buying low," but almost no one agrees on what "low" actually is. A falling price is not low. A discount is not a bargain. A stock down 30% is not automatically attractive, just as a stock at an all-time high is not automatically expensive. Price alone tells you nothing about opportunity.

To understand what "low" truly means, you must first understand the Law of Value. Price is what the market offers you in this moment. Value is what the asset is fundamentally worth based on earnings power, cash flow durability, competitive strength, and long-term relevance. Wealth is created in the space between these two numbers — the gap where fear pushes price below value.

Markets misprice assets far more often than people assume. They do so because markets are emotional. Panic, sudden shocks, forced liquidations, herd behaviour, and overreactions routinely push prices to irrational extremes. In those moments, assets with strong fundamentals trade as if they are broken, simply because sentiment overwhelms logic. These are the moments where disciplined investors find their edge.

Real "low" emerges from a specific combination of conditions:

Strong fundamentals + Temporary fear + Valuation discount

If all three conditions align, you are not simply looking at a cheap price — you are looking at a mispriced opportunity.

This chapter will teach you how to recognize and measure that opportunity with clarity. You will learn how to evaluate fundamentals, how to judge whether fear is temporary or structural, and how to determine whether the current price offers a genuine margin of safety. You will also learn why insiders and institutional buyers often step in during these moments of fear — and why tracking their behaviour helps you identify true LOW zones.

To make this practical, we introduce the **Low Zone Checklist**, a simple but powerful diagnostic tool:

- **Undervalued:** Price trades 20–70% below conservative fair value.
- **Fundamentals intact:** Core business or asset quality remains strong.
- **Fear-driven decline:** Selling is emotional, not structural.
- **Smart money buying:** Insiders or institutions are accumulating.

This chapter will show you how to apply these principles across stocks, crypto, real estate, commodities, and indices. Once you understand what "low" truly means, you will never look at market drops the same way again — you will see the structure behind the chaos, and the opportunities hidden within it.

1.1 Price vs. Value

Most people enter markets believing price and value are the same. They watch prices rise and assume value is rising. They see prices fall and assume value is falling. This misunderstanding is the root of most investment mistakes.

Price is loud. Value is quiet.

Price moves second by second; value evolves slowly over months or years.

Price reacts to emotion; value responds to fundamentals.

Price is a negotiation; value is an assessment.

Price is what you pay.
Value is what the asset is worth.

The difference between these two numbers—whether small or enormous—is where every opportunity and every risk in markets is born.

Why Price Is Not a Signal

Price contains information, but not all information is meaningful. A falling price can indicate one of two very different realities:

1. Something genuinely bad has happened and value has dropped.
2. Nothing fundamental has changed, and the market is overreacting.

Without understanding value, you cannot tell the difference. You cannot know whether a falling price is a bargain or a trap. You cannot know whether a rising price is justified growth or euphoric speculation. Price alone blinds you. Value gives you sight.

The Nature of Value

Value is anchored in fundamentals. It reflects:

- Earnings power and cash flow generation
- Asset quality and competitive advantage
- Balance sheet strength and debt stability
- Demand durability for the product or service
- Management quality and strategic direction
- Long-term structural tailwinds or headwinds

Value does not fluctuate because of a two-day news cycle or a viral post. It moves when the underlying reality of the asset changes. This slow, deliberate nature of value is exactly what creates the opportunity: markets move fast, fundamentals move slow. When price moves much faster than value, mispricing emerges.

Mispricing: The Source of All Opportunity

Every great investor—Graham, Buffett, Templeton, Lynch, Soros—built their edge on the recognition that price frequently detaches from value.

This detachment happens because markets are human systems. They overreact, extrapolate, panic, celebrate, fear, and herd. These behavioral dynamics create temporary distortions. When fear inflates the gap between price and value on the downside, you find opportunity. When euphoria stretches the gap on the upside, you find risk.

Wealth is created in the gap between price and value.

When price falls while value remains stable, the gap becomes positive. When price rises far above value, the gap becomes negative.

Your objective as an investor is not to predict price. Your objective is to understand value, observe the gap, and act when the difference becomes irrational.

How the Gap Becomes a Strategy

The entire discipline of buying low and selling high is built on one equation:

$$\textbf{Buy when Price} < \textbf{Value}$$
$$\textbf{Sell when Price} > \textbf{Value}$$

This is not a poetic phrase; it is a mechanical rule:

- If price is below value, you are buying future upside at a discount.
- If price is above value, you are paying a premium for emotion or narrative.
- If price equals value, the market is fairly balanced.

This simple framework explains why a 50% crash in a strong business can be a once-in-a-decade opportunity, and why a 300% rally in a weak business can be a prelude to disaster.

Why Most People Fail to Separate Price and Value

Most investors never develop a valuation mindset because:

1. **Price is easier to observe.** It is immediate, clear, and requires no thinking.
2. **Value requires analysis.** It demands judgment, patience, and a process.
3. **Humans love shortcuts.** Headlines, hype, and recent returns feel more actionable.
4. **Markets amplify emotion.** When everyone reacts to price, it becomes harder to think independently.

But the cost of ignoring value is enormous: you end up buying excitement and selling fear—the exact opposite of intelligent investing.

The Practical Implication

Understanding price versus value changes your behavior:

- You no longer panic during crashes—you investigate.
- You no longer chase rallies—you evaluate.
- You no longer rely on predictions—you rely on fundamentals.
- You no longer ask, "Why is the price falling?" You ask, "Has the value changed?"

This mindset shift is the foundation of all intelligent decision-making in markets. Without it, the rest of this book cannot help you. With it, the entire framework becomes powerful.

A Simple Thought Experiment

Imagine a business worth $100 based on cash flows, assets, and competitive strength. If the market price crashes to $60 because of temporary fear, the value remains $100. You have a $40 gap—a 40% margin of opportunity.

Now imagine the opposite. The market pushes the price to $160 because of hype and narrative while value remains $100. You have a $60 gap—but this time, it is a margin of risk, not opportunity.

This is why disciplined investors focus relentlessly on the gap, not the noise around the price.

The Core Behavior This Section Builds

Once you internalize the difference between price and value, you stop asking surface-level questions ("Is the stock going up?"). You start asking deeper ones:

- "What is this business worth?"
- "What is driving recent price action?"
- "Is this decline temporary or structural?"
- "What assumptions are baked into the price?"
- "Is the market reacting emotionally?"

The rest of this chapter builds on this foundation. The next sections will show you why markets misprice, how these gaps emerge, how to measure value conservatively, and how to identify true LOW zones with precision.

Once you master price versus value, you become insulated against noise. You stop reacting to markets—and start understanding them.

1.2 Why Markets Misprice

If markets were perfectly rational, buying low and selling high would be impossible. Every asset would always trade at its true value, leaving no gaps to exploit and no opportunities for outperformance. Fortunately—and predictably—markets are not rational systems. They are emotional, reactive, and frequently chaotic human ecosystems.

Mispricing happens because people, not equations, drive markets. And people carry emotions, biases, imperfect information, and uneven incentives. This creates persistent gaps between price and value, and those gaps are where disciplined investors build their edge.

Below are the dominant forces that repeatedly push prices away from fair value.

1. Emotion: The Primary Driver of Short-Term Prices

Emotion is the single biggest force behind mispricing. Prices often move not because fundamentals change, but because feelings do.

Fear causes investors to sell the moment something appears uncertain. **Greed** leads them to buy simply because price is rising.

These emotional reactions happen faster than rational analysis. Markets, especially liquid ones, reflect collective emotion almost instantly. A single headline can cause billions of dollars to move in minutes—not because value changed, but because people felt something.

Emotional waves create irrational lows and irrational highs.

2. Panic: When Fear Becomes Contagious

Panic is fear amplified. It happens when investors assume the worst possible outcome and rush to protect themselves. Panic selling is rarely about fundamentals; it is about survival instinct.

Examples include:

- sudden market crashes,
- unexpected geopolitical events,
- regulatory shocks,
- liquidity freezes,
- rumors spreading faster than truth.

In panic, investors no longer ask, "What is this worth?" They ask, "How do I exit right now?"

This desperation pushes price far below value, often dramatically. These are the moments where great investors quietly accumulate.

3. Overreaction: When the Market Exaggerates News

Markets swing like a pendulum—rarely stopping in the middle.

Good news gets exaggerated. Bad news gets magnified.

A company missing earnings by 2% can see its stock fall 20%. A small regulatory filing can cause widespread fear. A CEO comment can ignite a rally far beyond what fundamentals justify.

This happens because:

- investors extrapolate small events into large stories,
- traders speculate on short-term momentum,
- algorithms amplify moves once thresholds break,
- media dramatizes minor developments,

- retail investors pile in without context.

Overreaction pushes prices away from fair value—not slowly, but violently. Understanding this helps you recognize when a discount is temporary, not fundamental.

4. Herd Mentality: The Crowd's Illusion of Safety

Humans have evolved to follow the group. In markets, this instinct becomes dangerous.

Herd mentality makes investors act not from independent thought, but from social pressure:

- buying because "everyone else is buying,"
- selling because "everyone else is selling,"
- joining trends out of FOMO,
- avoiding positions because "the market must know something."

The crowd is often right in the middle of a trend, but almost always wrong at turning points.

The herd buys at the top from euphoria and sells at the bottom from fear. This collective behavior creates extreme mispricing in both directions.

5. Liquidity Shocks: When Forced Selling Breaks Logic

Sometimes prices drop not because investors want to sell, but because they are **forced** to sell. These liquidity-driven events create some of the most dramatic and short-lived misprices.

Examples:

- Margin calls triggering automatic selling
- Funds liquidating positions to meet investor redemptions
- Leverage unwind events
- Collateral failures
- Algorithmic liquidations in crypto

Liquidity shocks are mechanical, not fundamental. They create sudden drops that have nothing to do with the real value of the asset.

These moments are uncomfortable to watch but profoundly profitable for prepared investors.

Why These Forces Matter

These five forces—emotion, panic, overreaction, herd mentality, and liquidity shocks—share a common trait:

They move price quickly, but they almost never change value.

When these forces appear, the gap between price and value widens. That widening gap is the foundation of every "buy low" opportunity in markets.

Understanding why mispricing happens gives you the courage to act when others freeze, the patience to wait when others rush, and the clarity to distinguish temporary fear from real long-term risk.

This chapter will build on this foundation to help you identify true LOW zones with confidence and precision.

1.3 The Definition of LOW

Every investor hears the phrase "buy low," but almost no one knows how to define what "low" actually is. A price drop alone does not qualify. A 20% correction does not make something low. Even a 50% crash does not automatically make an asset a bargain.

"Low" is not a number. It is a **condition** — a specific alignment of value, fundamentals, and sentiment.

To invest intelligently, you must separate what merely looks cheap from what is *truly undervalued*. This requires a structured definition.

LOW = Strong fundamentals + Temporary fear + Valuation discount

If any one of these elements is missing, the opportunity is incomplete. If all three align, you have entered a zone where risk decreases and potential return increases.

Let's break down each component in depth.

1. Strong Fundamentals: The Core That Must Hold

A low price is only attractive if the underlying asset remains healthy. Fundamentals are the backbone of value—they tell you what the asset can earn, sustain, and grow over time.

Strong fundamentals mean:

- revenues and cash flows remain stable or recoverable,
- debt levels are manageable,
- competitive position is intact,

- demand for the product or asset remains long-term viable,
- management remains competent and aligned.

In other words, the business or asset must still possess the qualities that made it valuable in the first place.

A price decline due to temporary sentiment is an opportunity. A price decline due to permanent fundamental deterioration is a warning.

2. Temporary Fear: The Emotional Catalyst for Mispricing

Panic, overreaction, and uncertainty temporarily push prices far below what the asset is truly worth. The key word is **temporary**.

Temporary fear includes:

- sector-wide panic,
- macro shocks (inflation scares, interest rate surprises),
- sentiment-driven sell-offs,
- false rumors or misunderstood news,
- liquidity-driven events where forced selling occurs.

These events create an emotional wave that depresses price without significantly affecting long-term fundamentals. This is how mispricing forms.

If fear is structural—such as technological disruption or business model collapse—then it is not "low"; it is a value trap.

3. Valuation Discount: The Mathematical Proof of Opportunity

Even if fundamentals are strong and fear is temporary, you still need one more element: **a price that trades well below a conservative estimate of fair value.**

This discount is the margin of safety. It compensates for uncertainty and gives your investment room for error.

A valuation discount typically looks like:

- 20–70% below conservative fair-value estimates,
- significantly cheaper than peers on multiples,
- historically attractive relative to the asset's own valuation ranges,
- yielding unusually high cash-flow returns (earnings yield, FCF yield),
- priced below intrinsic replacement or liquidation cost (in hard assets).

The deeper the discount, the larger the opportunity—as long as the fundamentals remain strong.

Why All Three Must Come Together

It is common to find one or two elements of the LOW definition. But true opportunity arises only when all three align.

- **Strong fundamentals + valuation discount, but no fear:** Price may stay discounted for a long time; no catalyst.
- **Valuation discount + fear, but weak fundamentals:** This is a value trap.
- **Strong fundamentals + fear, but no valuation discount:** Emotional noise, but not a buying opportunity.

The LOW zone emerges **only** when:

1. Fundamentals ensure safety.
2. Fear creates mispricing.
3. Valuation provides a mathematical edge.

This trifecta produces asymmetric opportunity—where your downside risk is limited, but your upside potential is large.

LOW as a Psychological Advantage

Understanding this definition gives you confidence when the crowd is panicking. Most investors see red and run. You will see red and investigate.

Because you know:

- temporary fear is emotional, not structural,
- the business remains solid beneath the chaos,
- the discount is mathematically compelling.

This is the mindset of disciplined investors. They buy when value exceeds price—not when price feels comfortable.

The Practical Outcome

Once you internalize the definition of LOW, your behavior changes:

- You stop guessing bottoms and start recognizing value.
- You stop chasing prices and start analyzing fundamentals.
- You stop fearing declines and start seeing opportunity.
- You stop listening to panic and start listening to math.

The rest of this chapter—and the entire BL-SH framework—builds on this foundation. Everything begins with defining LOW correctly.

Only then can you buy low with confidence.

1.4 The Low Zone Checklist

Identifying a true LOW zone is not guesswork. It is not about catching falling knives or predicting bottoms. It is a structured, evidence-based assessment of whether an asset is trading below its true worth for reasons that are temporary, emotional, or mechanically forced.

The Low Zone Checklist distills this process into four objective conditions. Only when all four are present should you consider entering a position with conviction.

1. Undervalued: Price Trades 20–70% Below Fair Value

The first condition of a LOW zone is a **meaningful valuation discount**. A 5–10% dip is normal market noise. Even a 15% drop may not signal opportunity. Real LOW zones emerge when price trades well below a conservative fair-value range.

A practical range is:

- **20–40% discount:** moderate dislocation, early accumulation range,
- **40–70% discount:** deep value compression, high-opportunity zone,
- **70%+ discount:** extreme panic or forced liquidation (rare, but powerful).

This valuation gap can be identified using:

- conservative valuation models (PE, EV/EBITDA, FCF yield),
- historical multiples relative to the business's norms,
- peer comparisons adjusted for quality and risk,
- asset-based or replacement-cost analysis in real estate and commodities,
- discounted cash flow estimates using conservative assumptions.

The deeper the discount—*as long as the fundamentals are intact*—the more asymmetric the opportunity becomes.

2. Fundamentals Intact: The Core Must Still Be Strong

A low price is only attractive if the underlying business or asset remains healthy. Fundamentals are the anchor that distinguishes a bargain from a value trap.

Fundamentals are considered intact if:

- the business continues generating stable or recovering cash flow,
- the balance sheet is healthy (manageable leverage, sufficient liquidity),

- the product or asset retains long-term relevance,
- competitive advantages remain unchanged,
- management quality and accountability remain visible,
- structural demand is unaffected by the temporary shock.

You must confirm that:

- the decline is not due to permanent margin collapse,
- the business model is not being replaced,
- technology is not rendering the product obsolete,
- regulations are not permanently harming the economics.

If fundamentals are deteriorating structurally, the price is not low—it is fair or even high relative to the future. True LOW zones require durability beneath the chaos.

3. Fear-Driven Sell-Off: Temporary, Emotional, or Mechanical Decline

A LOW zone almost always appears in the middle of an emotional storm. Prices fall sharply because investors are reacting to fear, uncertainty, or forced selling—not because long-term value has collapsed.

Common fear-driven catalysts include:

- macro shocks (inflation spikes, interest-rate scares),
- sector-wide panic from unrelated news,
- negative headlines that are misunderstood or exaggerated,
- short-term earnings disappointment with no impact on long-term value,
- liquidity crunches (margin calls, redemptions, forced unwinds),
- algorithmic selling during volatility spikes,
- market-wide risk-off sentiment.

The key markers of a fear-driven decline are:

- price drops faster than fundamentals change,
- volume spikes without corresponding deterioration in business metrics,
- analysts downgrade based on emotion rather than structural analysis,
- investors sell "just to feel safe," not because value changed.

Fear-driven sell-offs create **temporary mispricing**, which is the foundation of a LOW zone. Your job is to differentiate temporary turbulence from permanent impairment.

4. Insider or Institutional Accumulation: Smart Money Behavior

One of the most powerful signals confirming a LOW zone is the behavior of investors who know the asset best.

Insiders (executives, founders, board members) **Institutions** (long-term funds, pensions, sovereign funds)

When price collapses but fundamentals remain intact, these players often use the moment to accumulate shares quietly. They understand long-term value better than the general public and often act when the crowd is fearful.

Evidence of smart-money accumulation includes:

- insider buying filings increasing,
- institutions raising positions during sell-offs,
- stable or rising ownership by long-term value-focused funds,
- reduction in short interest,
- increased block trades at depressed prices.

Smart money does not chase hype. It buys when assets are unloved, undervalued, and misunderstood.

How the Checklist Protects You

The Low Zone Checklist converts chaos into clarity. It ensures you do not buy simply because price fell. It forces discipline by requiring:

1. a mathematical edge (valuation discount),
2. a fundamental safety net (durable business),
3. a psychological filter (fear-driven, not structural decline),
4. a confirmation signal (smart-money support).

If all four align, probability shifts in your favor. Your downside risk shrinks, and your upside potential expands.

The Low Zone Is Not Guessing—It Is Diagnosis

With this checklist, you do not attempt to pick bottoms. You identify conditions where:

- price is dislocated from value,
- the fundamentals justify ownership,
- the emotional storm is temporary,

- informed capital validates your thesis.

This is how disciplined investors buy low—not by prediction, but by structured recognition of mispricing.

The rest of this chapter will show you how to apply this checklist using real examples and how to avoid value traps that look cheap but fail these conditions.

1.5 Real Examples of LOW Zones

LOW zones are not theoretical. They appear repeatedly across sectors, countries, and decades. They occur when fundamentals remain intact, but sentiment collapses and valuation disconnects from reality. This section shows four powerful examples where fear created extraordinary opportunity.

1. Apple (2013): A $400 Stock Everyone Thought Was Finished

In 2013, Apple entered one of its most misunderstood periods. The stock fell nearly 45%, dropping from around $700 (pre-split) to under $400.

Why the Market Panicked:

- Media claimed Apple had "lost innovation."
- Concerns around slowing iPhone sales.
- Fear that Android would destroy Apple's ecosystem.
- Analysts predicted margins would collapse.

But Fundamentals Remained Strong:

- Record revenue and cash flow.
- Massive global ecosystem expansion.
- High customer loyalty and brand power.
- Billions in cash reserves.
- High-margin services starting to grow.

Valuation Became Absurdly Low:

- Apple traded at a single-digit P/E.
- Market priced Apple like a dying hardware company.
- Intrinsic value far above market price.

LOW-Zone Snapshot:

- Strong fundamentals
- Temporary fear
- Valuation discount

The result? Apple went on to become a multi-trillion-dollar company — rewarding anyone who recognized the LOW zone.

2. Bitcoin (2018): Fear Without Fundamental Damage

After Bitcoin's 2017 rise, the asset crashed nearly 85% during 2018. The entire world declared Bitcoin dead.

Fear-Dominated Narrative:

- "Crypto will go to zero."
- "It was all a bubble."
- Daily headlines predicting collapse.
- Retail panic selling everywhere.

But the Fundamentals of the Network Stayed Intact:

- Hash rate kept increasing.
- Developer activity remained strong.
- Institutional interest quietly grew.
- Long-term holders accumulated.
- Bitcoin's monetary design unchanged.

Valuation Disconnected from Reality:

- Price fell faster than network value.
- Sentiment completely decoupled from fundamentals.
- Classic capitulation pattern.

LOW-Zone Characteristics Clearly Present:

- Extreme fear
- Strong fundamentals (network + code)
- Deep valuation discount

Within three years, Bitcoin rebounded from $3,500 to over $60,000 — a textbook LOW-zone example.

3. Google (2022): Cloud Fears and "Big Tech Is Finished" Narratives

In 2022, markets punished tech stocks heavily, and Google (Alphabet) dropped 40%.

The Fear Narrative:

- Ads slowdown due to recession fears.
- Rising inflation and interest rates.
- Concerns that YouTube growth was flattening.
- Anxiety about competition from TikTok and AI.

But Google's Core Engine Was Untouched:

- Dominant search business still printing cash.
- Cloud division growing aggressively.
- Massive free cash flow.
- Zero threat to the core business model.
- Strong balance sheet, minimal debt.

Valuation Dropped to Rare Historic Lows:

- P/E compressed to near "recession levels."
- Market priced Google as if decline was permanent.

LOW-Zone Signals:

- Sentiment extremely negative
- Fundamentals intact
- Valuation significantly below fair value

Within a year, Google rebounded sharply — again proving that fear creates mispricing.

4. Real Estate (2020): COVID Rental Panic

In early 2020, global real estate markets saw an extreme panic due to COVID and lockdowns.

The Fear:

- Tenant defaults.
- Rent holidays.

- Retail properties shut for months.
- Offices viewed as "obsolete forever."
- Predictions of a 40–60% long-term collapse.

Fundamentals Didn't Collapse:

- Housing demand stayed structurally strong.
- Mortgage rates fell due to central bank action.
- Remote work stabilized income for many households.
- Institutional investors stepped in aggressively.
- Long-term supply remained tight in major cities.

Valuation Discounts Appeared Everywhere:

- REITs trading 30–60% below NAV.
- High-quality rental properties sold at distressed prices.
- Markets mispriced temporary disruption as permanent destruction.

LOW-Zone Snapshot:

- Temporary panic
- Underlying demand intact
- Big discount to intrinsic value

Real estate rebounded strongly once the panic faded — confirming this as another classic LOW zone.

Summary

Across Apple, Bitcoin, Google, and real estate, one pattern repeats:

Fear creates the discount. Fundamentals create the opportunity.

LOW zones feel uncomfortable when they happen — but they produce the greatest long-term returns when recognized with discipline.

Key Takeaways

- **Price and value are not the same.** Price reflects emotion, noise, and short-term sentiment. Value reflects fundamentals, durability, and long-term worth.
- **Wealth is created in the gap between price and value.** Opportunity appears when price falls faster than value, and risk appears when price rises faster than value.
- **Markets misprice because humans misreact.** Emotion, panic, overreaction, herd behavior, and liquidity shocks regularly push prices away from fair value.
- **"Low" is not a price level—it is a condition.** A falling price does not make an asset low unless value remains intact.
- **The TRUE definition of LOW is:**

  Strong fundamentals + Temporary fear + Valuation discount

  All three must align to create a genuine BUY zone.
- **Undervaluation requires a meaningful discount.** Price is typically 20–70% below conservative fair value during a real LOW zone.
- **Fundamentals must be intact.** A LOW zone exists only if the business or asset remains strong, stable, and capable of long-term performance.
- **Fear-driven sell offs create temporary mispricing.** Emotional or mechanical selling—not structural damage— creates the conditions for opportunity.
- **Smart-money accumulation validates the thesis.** Insider or institutional buying during a decline is one of the strongest confirmations of true undervaluation.
- **The Low Zone Checklist prevents emotional mistakes.** It ensures that you buy based on evidence, not fear, and that you avoid value traps that only appear cheap.
- **Identifying LOW is a skill, not luck.** With valuation, fundamentals, sentiment analysis, and smart-money signals, buying low becomes a repeatable method.

The next chapter builds on these foundations by showing how to identify the opposite condition—the HIGH zone where price exceeds value, emotions turn euphoric, and disciplined investors prepare to exit.

Chapter 2

The Law of Euphoria: What High Really Means

Introduction

If the Law of Value teaches us what "low" truly means, then the Law of Euphoria reveals the opposite side of the cycle—when prices detach from reality, emotions drive decisions, and markets enter the danger zone disguised as opportunity.

Most investors believe that "high" simply means a high price. But a price can be high for the right reasons—strong earnings, expanding markets, sustainable growth. A price becomes dangerously high only when it rises far beyond what fundamentals can justify. Euphoria is not about the number on the screen; it is about the psychology behind that number.

High = Overvaluation + Mania + Narrative Excess

This is the core definition of a HIGH zone. It is a state where price accelerates faster than value, where optimism converts into delusion, and where stories overpower statistics. In these moments, investors stop asking "What is this worth?" and begin asking "How much higher can it go?"—a question that has marked the beginning of every major market peak in history.

The purpose of this chapter is to give you a clean, precise contrast to the LOW zone you studied earlier. Just as LOW is a structural opportunity created by fear, HIGH is a structural risk created by euphoria. Understanding this distinction will protect you from overpaying, chasing hype, or getting trapped at the top of a mania.

To make "high" practical and measurable, we introduce the **High Zone Checklist**, a diagnostic tool that reveals when an asset has entered dangerous territory:

- **Valuation stretched:** price trades dramatically above conservative fair-value ranges.

- **Parabolic price rise:** the chart goes vertical—an unmistakable sign of unsustainable acceleration.
- **Euphoric sentiment:** investors become certain, overconfident, and dismissive of risk.
- **Insider selling or institutional distribution:** informed players exit while the crowd buys.

Just like LOW zones have patterns, HIGH zones have their own unmistakable fingerprints:

- **Headlines everywhere:** media celebrates the asset as unstoppable.
- **Social media buzz:** influencers, forums, and new traders promote it aggressively.
- **"This time it's different" narratives:** the most dangerous sentence in finance.
- **New beginners entering at peak:** late, inexperienced buyers flood in at the worst moment.

Euphoria is powerful because it feels good. Prices rise, everyone seems to be making money, and doubt feels like weakness. But euphoria is also fragile. When price rises for emotional reasons, it collapses just as easily when emotions reverse. Recognizing the signs of HIGH is one of the most important skills in long-term wealth building—not only to protect gains, but to avoid catastrophic losses.

This chapter will teach you how to spot overvaluation, detect euphoric behavior, interpret parabolic charts, and read institutional exit activity. You will learn the subtle signals that appear before peaks, the narrative traps that seduce beginners, and the precise conditions under which disciplined investors begin to reduce exposure.

Just as the Law of Value revealed where opportunities are born, the Law of Euphoria reveals where risks hide in plain sight.

2.1 Why "High" Is Not Just a High Price

Most investors mistakenly believe that an asset becomes "high" simply because its price has risen. But a rising price alone does not create danger. A business can grow, earnings can expand, cash flows can accelerate, and value can rise accordingly. In such cases, a higher price is justified. It reflects progress, not euphoria.

The real problem begins when price rises faster than value. When price detaches from fundamentals. When optimism turns into mania. When stories overpower statistics.

A price becomes "high" not because the number is large, but because the *gap* between price and value becomes dangerously wide.

High = Overvaluation + Mania + Narrative Excess

This formula is the essence of every market top in history. It transforms a simple observation ("price went up") into a diagnostic condition that signals: *risk is rising, liquidity is thinning, and the crowd is losing judgment.*

Let's break this down.

1. Overvaluation: When Expectations Outrun Reality

Overvaluation happens when price reflects a future that is too optimistic to be realistic. Markets begin to assume perfect execution, endless growth, and zero friction. Instead of valuing what the business is, investors value what they hope it will become.

Signs of overvaluation include:

- valuation multiples expanding beyond historical norms,
- price rising significantly faster than earnings or cash flow,
- analysts justifying high prices using stretched or unrealistic assumptions,
- investors believing traditional metrics "no longer apply."

Overvaluation alone is dangerous, but not yet euphoric. It becomes truly risky when psychology enters the equation.

2. Mania: When Behavior Detaches From Logic

Mania is the emotional fuel behind every unsustainable rally. This is when investors stop asking questions and start accepting narratives blindly. Mania is characterized by:

- rapid inflows from retail investors,
- accelerating trading volumes,
- buy-the-dip becoming automatic, not analytical,
- belief that "it can only go up,"
- fear not of loss, but of missing out (FOMO).

During mania, price becomes a self-fulfilling prophecy. Rising prices attract new buyers, which cause prices to rise further, pulling in even more buyers. This is a feedback loop, not a valuation process.

Mania replaces uncertainty with overconfidence. That shift is what pushes assets into the HIGH zone.

3. Narrative Excess: When Stories Replace Facts

Narratives are powerful. They give investors something to believe in. But narratives become dangerous when they drift too far from reality. Narrative excess appears when:

- headlines praise the asset as unstoppable,
- influencers and media push simplified "get-in-now" messages,
- investors repeat slogans rather than analysis,
- caution is dismissed as ignorance,
- any criticism is labeled as "not understanding the future."

The most dangerous sentence in finance —

"This time it's different."

Narrative excess turns temporary enthusiasm into unsustainable valuation. It is the psychological bridge between overvaluation and mania.

Why This Matters

A high price does not mean risk. A euphoric price does.

A fundamentally strong business can rise 50% and still be fairly valued. A mediocre business can rise 50% and become wildly overvalued.

The difference is not the price movement — *it is the force behind the movement.*

By understanding that "high" is not a number but a condition, you avoid chasing hype, avoid buying into manias, and avoid becoming liquidity for insiders exiting at the peak.

In Summary

Price becomes "high" when three forces converge:

1. **Overvaluation:** price outruns fundamentals,
2. **Mania:** emotions outrun logic,
3. **Narrative excess:** stories outrun reality.

This is the High Zone. This is where caution is required. This is where risk becomes invisible but enormous.

The next section introduces the **High Zone Checklist**, a structured method to identify these danger signals with precision.

2.2 The High Zone Checklist

Recognizing when an asset has entered the HIGH zone is just as important as identifying LOW zones. If LOW represents opportunity born from fear, HIGH represents danger born from euphoria. This checklist gives you a structured way to diagnose when an asset is no longer priced for reality, but for fantasy.

A HIGH zone is not about a high number — it is about a dangerous combination of stretched valuation, overheated price action, psychological excess, and smart money quietly exiting.

Below are the four essential components of a true HIGH zone. All four do not need to appear, but the more that align, the larger the risk.

1. Valuation Stretched: Price Detached From Fundamentals

Valuation becomes stretched when price exceeds even optimistic estimates of fair value. At this stage, investors are no longer buying the business or asset — they are buying expectations, narratives, and speculative momentum.

Signs of stretched valuation:

- valuation multiples far above historical norms,
- price rising much faster than earnings or cash flow,
- analysts raising targets based on momentum, not fundamentals,
- investors believing traditional metrics no longer matter,
- discounted cash flow models requiring unrealistic assumptions,
- asset priced as if perfection is guaranteed indefinitely.

When valuation stretches too far, the elastic snaps. This is usually the earliest sign of a HIGH zone forming.

2. Parabolic Price Rise: Vertical, Unsustainable Acceleration

Parabolic price action is one of the clearest and most reliable signatures of euphoria. Instead of rising steadily, prices begin to accelerate vertically — faster and faster over shorter time periods.

Characteristics of a parabolic move:

- sharp, near-vertical price rises on charts,
- multiple large green candles with minimal pullbacks,
- relentless buying pressure regardless of news or fundamentals,

- re-acceleration after each dip (dip-buying mania),
- massive increase in trading volume,
- new investors rushing in simply because "it keeps going up."

Parabolic moves do not end softly. They end violently — usually with equally sharp reversals. Recognizing them early protects your gains when others are blinded by momentum.

3. Euphoric Sentiment: When Investors Stop Thinking

Euphoria is not optimism — it is the suspension of skepticism. It is the belief that risk no longer exists, that the asset will rise indefinitely, and that any hesitation is foolish.

Indicators of euphoric sentiment:

- investors discussing price targets without rationale,
- social media filled with celebratory posts, not analysis,
- "get in now or be left behind" messaging,
- people increasing position size emotionally, not strategically,
- retail traders leveraging up to chase the move,
- the disappearance of dissenting opinions.

Euphoria creates a psychological bubble. It convinces people that rising prices are proof of value — when in reality, they are only proof of psychology.

4. Insider Selling / Institutional Distribution: Smart Money Exits

One of the most powerful and reliable signals of a HIGH zone is the behavior of those who know the asset best. When insiders or institutions begin reducing their positions, it usually means they believe the price has exceeded reasonable value.

Forms of smart-money distribution:

- corporate insiders selling shares after a rapid price rise,
- large institutions quietly trimming exposure,
- declining institutional ownership during a rally,
- increased block trades at or near peak levels,
- lock-up expirations used aggressively to cash out,
- insider selling concentrated near all-time highs.

Insiders and institutions rarely buy into mania — they sell into it. Their activity is a mirror to the emotions of the crowd.

The Power of the Checklist

When these four elements align, the probability of a peak becomes extremely high:

1. **Valuation has outrun fundamentals.** The numbers cannot justify the price.
2. **Price has entered a vertical, unsustainable trajectory.** Momentum has replaced logic.
3. **Sentiment has shifted from excitement to euphoria.** Risk is being ignored, not analyzed.
4. **Smart money is exiting while amateurs are entering.** Professionals are selling; beginners are buying.

This checklist is not about predicting exact tops. It is about identifying when *risk becomes asymmetrically high.* At this stage, the prudent action is to reduce exposure, tighten stops, or exit entirely.

Using the Checklist With Discipline

The High Zone Checklist protects you from:

- chasing parabolic moves,
- buying into hype-driven rallies,
- holding too long during mania,
- becoming liquidity for insider exits,
- mistaking popularity for value.

Just as the Low Zone Checklist reveals opportunity, the High Zone Checklist reveals danger.

The next section will teach you how to recognize the patterns that usually appear just before the peak — the signals hidden in media, social sentiment, and investor behavior that tell you euphoria has reached its climax.

2.3 Recognition Patterns

One of the most powerful ways to avoid buying at the top is to learn how peaks *look* and *feel.* High zones are rarely subtle. They announce themselves loudly through cultural, emotional, and behavioral signals.

These recognition patterns are universal. They appear in crypto, stocks, midcaps, blue-chips, commodities, and even real estate. Once you learn them, you can spot a peak forming long before price reverses.

This section explains the four major high-zone recognition patterns you will see again and again.

1. Headlines Everywhere

When an asset enters a euphoric phase, the media amplifies it endlessly.

You will see:

- daily headlines about new highs,
- aggressive price targets from analysts,
- stories celebrating investors who became rich overnight,
- constant coverage on TV, interviews, and news panels.

The media does not create the mania — it reflects and magnifies the emotional state of the crowd.

When an asset that was once ignored suddenly becomes a daily headline, you must ask: **Is this information, or is this sentiment?**

In high zones, headlines are not informational. They are emotional accelerants.

2. Social Media Buzz

Social platforms act as real-time sentiment sensors. When an asset hits peak euphoria, the noise becomes deafening.

Recognition signs:

- explosive increase in memes, fan pages, and hype posts,
- inexperienced accounts giving "expert" advice,
- extreme FOMO-driven comments,
- viral content predicting unrealistic future returns,
- influencers pushing the asset without understanding fundamentals.

Social media turns into a feedback loop:

Rising price → hype → more buyers → rising price → more hype

This loop is always temporary — and its very intensity is a warning signal.

3. "This Time It's Different" Narratives

Every major market top in history has been justified with the same sentence:

"This time it's different."

These narratives appear when price has already outrun fundamentals, and the crowd needs a story to justify buying at elevated valuations.

Typical versions of this narrative:

- "This company is in a new paradigm."
- "Traditional valuation metrics don't matter anymore."
- "Competition will never catch up."
- "This asset will only go up from here."
- "Old rules don't apply to this new industry."

What makes these narratives dangerous is not that they are completely false — but that they are used to rationalize prices far beyond intrinsic value.

Narratives grow faster than fundamentals. And when narratives peak, price soon follows.

4. New Beginners Entering at the Peak

One of the most reliable indicators of a HIGH zone is the arrival of new, inexperienced investors.

Signs beginners are entering the market:

- relatives and friends who never discuss markets suddenly ask: "Should I buy this?"
- first-time investors opening demat/crypto accounts,
- people buying simply because "everyone else is making money,"
- late-stage FOMO driving massive inflows,
- newcomers convinced that risk is low and rewards are guaranteed.

When new investors rush in after a huge rally, it usually means the cycle is near its final stage.

The same people who were afraid to buy during fear become eager to buy during euphoria. This behavior is reliable, predictable, and extremely useful for spotting tops.

Why These Patterns Matter

High-zone recognition is not about prediction — it is about identifying emotional overheating.

When you see:

- media obsession,
- social media hype,
- perfect narratives,
- and mass beginner participation,

you are no longer in rational valuation territory. You are in behavioral territory — a zone where risk grows exponentially while potential reward shrinks rapidly.

When everyone is excited, disciplined investors get cautious.

2.4 Case Studies of Market Tops

Market peaks are never random. They follow predictable emotional, psychological, and structural patterns. Although each asset has its own story, the *behavior* of tops is strikingly similar across time.

This section explores four famous HIGH-zone examples where euphoria, narrative excess, and parabolic price acceleration created some of the most dramatic market tops in history.

These case studies reinforce one truth:

Every bubble has different headlines, but the same human behavior underneath.

1. Dotcom Bubble (2000): When the Internet Made Valuation "Irrelevant"

The Dotcom Boom was one of the most classic HIGH zones in financial history. Technology stocks rose exponentially as investors believed the internet would rewrite every economic rule — instantly.

Recognition Signals at the Peak:

- Companies with no revenue or profits valued at billions.
- IPO mania — dozens of tech firms listed every month.
- Mainstream magazines declaring: "The Old Economy Is Dead."
- Parabolic rise in the NASDAQ index (100% in one year).
- Extreme retail participation, especially first-time investors.
- Analysts issuing absurd targets based on "eyeballs" and "clicks."

Why It Was a Clear HIGH Zone:

- Valuations were disconnected from fundamentals.
- Narratives became perfect — "every company will grow exponentially."
- Insiders and venture capital firms quietly sold into strength.
- Prices moved faster than technology adoption could justify.

What Happened Next:

- NASDAQ fell 78%.
- Thousands of tech companies disappeared.
- Only strong businesses (Amazon, Google) survived and grew.

This is the gold standard of HIGH-zone excess: **a perfect story + unlimited optimism + zero valuation discipline.**

2. Tesla (2020–2021): The Cult-Driven Euphoria

Tesla's 2020–2021 rally was one of the fastest and most emotional large-cap manias ever recorded. From a car company, Tesla transformed (in perception) into a "technology religion."

Signs of the HIGH Zone:

- Price rose more than 10× in under 18 months.
- Retail investors became extremely loyal and vocal ("TSLA to the moon").
- Media projected Tesla would dominate every global industry.
- Valuation reached 1,000× earnings at one point.
- Social media became a powerhouse of hype and price predictions.
- New investors entered only because "everyone is making money."
- Analysts stopped using traditional valuation metrics — "Tesla is a platform, not a car company."

Why It Was a HIGH Zone:

- Parabolic price acceleration.
- Narrative excess (AI + EV monopoly + robotics + energy domination).
- Institutions booked profits while retail increased exposure.
- Valuation stretched far beyond even optimistic scenarios.

Aftermath:

- Tesla experienced deep corrections of 50–70%.
- Fundamentals remained good, but price normalized from mania.
- Late entrants faced huge drawdowns.

Tesla is the perfect modern example of HIGH-zone psychology in a beloved stock.

3. Bitcoin (2021): The Perfect Storm of Euphoria

Bitcoin's 2021 rally was a textbook blend of:

- media hype,
- cultural momentum,
- institutional FOMO,
- and unrealistic price predictions.

Recognition Patterns at the Peak:

- Price surged from $10,000 to $69,000 in a year.
- Celebrities, athletes, and influencers endorsed crypto.
- Companies added "crypto" to their names to boost stock prices.
- NFTs and altcoins exploded with zero fundamentals.
- Retail investors borrowed money to buy dips.
- Extreme leverage in futures markets.

Why It Was a Clear HIGH Zone:

- Rapid price acceleration above fundamentals.
- "Bitcoin to $500k" predictions everywhere.
- New beginners entering the market with total confidence.
- Institutions selling into the retail-driven rally.
- Leverage overheating across the system.

What Followed:

- Bitcoin corrected 75%.
- Altcoins collapsed 90–99%.
- Leverage unwound painfully.

This was another classic HIGH zone: **narrative ¿ valuation, hype ¿ analysis, acceleration ¿ sustainability.**

4. Meme Stocks (GME & AMC, 2021): The Crowd Becomes the Market

The meme-stock mania was unique because it was not driven by fundamentals, but by collective social media emotion — especially Reddit's WallStreetBets.

Signs of High-Zone Mania:

- GME rose from $4 to $480 in weeks.
- AMC rose from pennies to over $70.
- Millions of new investors entered purely due to hype.
- "Diamond hands," "to the moon," and "hold at any cost" became slogans.
- No valuation metrics were discussed anywhere.
- Institutions used the spike to unload positions.

Why It Was Clearly a HIGH Zone:

- Pure narrative, no fundamentals.
- Parabolic price action.
- Social media feedback loops.
- Extreme FOMO and zero risk awareness.
- Liquidity surged only because of crowd excitement.

Aftermath:

- Both stocks collapsed 80–95%.
- Many retail investors lost huge amounts.
- Fundamentals eventually reasserted themselves.

Meme stocks are the clearest possible example of emotional buying at the top.

Summary

Across Dotcom, Tesla, Bitcoin, and Meme stocks, the same HIGH-zone forces appear:

Euphoria, narrative excess, media hype, parabolic price acceleration, and mass beginner entry.

Different assets. Different stories. Same human behavior.

Recognizing these patterns early is the key to avoiding tops — and executing Sell High with discipline.

Key Takeaways

- **Wealth is mathematical, not emotional.** Long-term results come from following a simple, mechanical law — not from luck, prediction, or constant market activity.

- **The Wealth Equation:**

  $$\text{Wealth} = (\text{Capital} \times \text{Accuracy} \times \text{Cycles Repeated})$$

  This formula explains all compounding across markets.

- **Capital is your base multiplier.** The more consistently you save, invest, and protect capital from large losses, the more powerful compounding becomes.

- **Accuracy does not require perfection.** You only need a system — like the BL–SH framework — that identifies LOW zones and HIGH zones more reliably than your emotions.

- **Repetition is the hidden exponent.** Wealth doesn't come from one great decision. It comes from repeating the right cycle — buy in fear, sell in euphoria — across many market phases.

- **You don't need to win every time.** Even 60–70% accuracy becomes extraordinary when applied over multiple cycles.

- **Avoiding catastrophic mistakes is more important than chasing perfect wins.** Surviving, staying disciplined, and staying invested matter far more than predicting tops and bottoms.

- **Emotions break the equation; systems activate it.** Mechanical, rule-based behavior compounds; emotional behavior destroys compounding.

- **The more cycles you repeat with accuracy, the faster wealth accelerates.** Compounding is not linear — it is exponential. Each cycle builds on the last.

This chapter turns wealth creation from a mystery into a predictable, repeatable process — a law you can follow for life.

Key Takeaways

- **A high price is not the danger — euphoria is.** Prices can rise for healthy reasons, but when price outruns value, risk becomes invisible and dangerous.
- **A true HIGH zone is a condition, not a number.** It appears when valuation, psychology, and narrative combine to push prices far above fundamental reality.
- **The definition of HIGH is:**

  $$\textbf{Overvaluation + Mania + Narrative Excess}$$

  All three forces together create unsustainable price levels.
- **Valuation becomes stretched when expectations exceed reality.** Multiples expand beyond reason, optimistic assumptions replace analysis, and price reflects perfection rather than probability.
- **Parabolic price action is one of the strongest danger signals.** Vertical, accelerating moves rarely sustain; they almost always reverse sharply.
- **Euphoric sentiment replaces caution with overconfidence.** Investors stop questioning risk, assume endless upside, and treat skepticism as ignorance — the classic setup for a peak.
- **Smart money exits while the crowd buys.** Insider selling and institutional distribution are powerful indications that those who know the asset best believe it is overpriced.
- **HIGH zones have recognizable patterns.** Media hype, viral social buzz, "this time it's different" narratives, and a surge of beginner participation typically appear near tops.
- **The High Zone Checklist protects capital.** It prevents you from chasing momentum, buying into mania, or holding too long when risk becomes asymmetric.
- **Recognizing HIGH is as important as recognizing LOW.** Selling high locks in gains, protects long-term returns, and prevents catastrophic drawdowns.

In the next chapter, we bring the two laws together and build the complete **Buy Low–Sell High Decision System** — the framework that integrates value, sentiment, psychology, and market structure into a repeatable method you can use across any asset class.

Chapter 3

The Market Cycle Map

Introduction

Markets do not move randomly. They move in cycles—repeating emotional, economic, and structural patterns that have played out across centuries, asset classes, and geographies. Whether you study stocks, crypto, real estate, commodities, or indices, the same rhythm appears again and again: fear turns into opportunity, opportunity turns into optimism, optimism turns into mania, and mania collapses into fear once more.

Understanding this rhythm is one of the most powerful skills in investing. Once you can identify where the market is in its cycle, you can predict the behavior of participants, the distortion of prices, and the opportunities or risks that lie ahead.

This chapter introduces the **Market Cycle Map**, a simplified, practical model that explains every phase of the market journey from the bottom to the top and back again. It shows you where LOW zones and HIGH zones naturally occur, and how investor psychology transforms as the cycle unfolds.

The complete cycle looks like this:

- **Accumulation (Stealth Buying, LOW Zone):** Prices are depressed, fear dominates, fundamentals are ignored, and only informed buyers quietly accumulate.
- **Early Uptick:** Value starts to assert itself, selling pressure fades, and prices begin rising slowly.
- **Momentum Phase:** Trend followers and early institutions join in; confidence grows and technical strength builds.
- **Public Participation:** The crowd discovers the asset. Media coverage increases. New investors enter.
- **Euphoria Peak (HIGH Zone):** Prices go parabolic. Narratives become extreme. Risk is invisible. Smart money exits.

- **Distribution:** Institutions quietly sell to late buyers. Momentum weakens beneath the surface.
- **Panic Crash:** Confidence breaks. Forced selling accelerates. Prices collapse faster than most expect.
- **Reset → Accumulation:** Fundamentals stabilize. Fear dominates again. The next cycle begins.

Every boom and bust in history—Dot-com 2000, Housing 2008, Bitcoin 2017, Oil 2020, Tech 2021—fits perfectly into this map. The labels change, the emotions do not.

At the heart of the Market Cycle Map lies one timeless rule:

Buy in fear-heavy early phases.
Sell in greed-heavy late phases.

This rule is simple but rarely followed because it goes against human nature. Fear blinds investors to opportunity; greed blinds them to risk.

This chapter will train you to see what others cannot during each stage: where value hides, where danger builds, and where true asymmetric decisions exist. By the end, you will be able to plot any asset—any timeframe—on the Market Cycle Map and act with clarity instead of emotion.

3.1 The Complete, Simplified Cycle

Markets move in repeating rhythms. Each cycle phase has distinct causes, participants, price action, and opportunities (or dangers). Below we walk through every phase in detail — what it looks like, why it happens, who participates, the common signals to watch, and the practical action you should consider as an investor. Learning these phases trains your eye to spot where value is hiding and where risk is growing.

1. Accumulation (Stealth Buying — LOW Zone)

What it is: The quiet bottom of the cycle. Prices are depressed or range-bound. Sentiment is negative. Most investors are pessimistic or indifferent. A small group of informed, long-term, or contrarian buyers (value funds, insiders, patient individuals) begin to accumulate.

Why it happens: Fear, recent losses, liquidity shocks, or temporary business setbacks push price below fair value while fundamentals remain intact or recoverable. Many sellers are forced or emotional; buyers who understand value quietly step in.

Who participates: Insiders (sometimes), long-only value managers, contrarian investors, founders adding when possible, opportunistic private buyers.

Common signals:

- Price near multi-month or multi-year lows.
- Elevated fear indicators (VIX, sentiment surveys).
- Stable or improving fundamentals despite price weakness.
- Insider buying or increasing institutional ownership.
- Low media coverage; the asset is unloved.

Practical action:

- Perform conservative valuation checks — look for margin of safety (20–50%+).
- Prepare a staged entry plan (initial small tranche + rules to add).
- Document the thesis: what would prove you right/wrong.
- Avoid large all-in bets; use optionality — small initial position with room to scale.

2. Early Uptick

What it is: The first sustained recovery from the bottom. Selling pressure eases, buyers return, and price trends slowly higher. This is the phase where quiet accumulation begins to show as price strength.

Why it happens: Early positive data, improving macro conditions, or signs that the worst is priced in lead cautious investors to re-enter. Market participants begin to re-evaluate the prior pessimism.

Who participates: Early adopters from the accumulation phase, nimble funds, some technicians noticing trend change, selective long-term buyers.

Common signals:

- Higher lows and modest higher highs on charts.
- Improving volume profile on up moves.
- Gradual reduction in headline negativity.
- Small upgrades by analysts or selective positive news.

Practical action:

- Add to initial positions according to your scale-in plan if value remains attractive.
- Tighten monitoring but keep a valuation-first lens — price movement is not yet broad participation.
- Use trailing alerts for re-entry if temporary pullbacks occur.

3. Momentum Phase

What it is: Price moves from cautious recovery into a sustained uptrend. Technical strength attracts trend-followers and momentum managers. Performance starts to look respectable on a relative basis.

Why it happens: As performance improves, more buyers join — technical funds, quant strategies, and news-driven flow — creating a reinforcing trend.

Who participates: Trend-following funds, momentum traders, selective institutions, and retail investors beginning to notice.

Common signals:

- Breakouts above key resistance levels (50/200-day moving averages).
- Rising relative strength versus peers or indices.
- Improving sentiment metrics and growing coverage.
- Increasing and steady volumes on up days.

Practical action:

- Continue to scale into positions if your value thesis still holds, but reduce the aggression of additions.
- Consider adding a small momentum allocation if your rules allow (strict sizing).
- Begin setting intermediate profit-taking rules for part of your position — you do not need to hold every share to ultimate victory.

4. Public Participation

What it is: The broader public discovers the asset. Headlines grow positive; retail influx increases; financial media runs stories. The market transitions from selective buying to widespread interest.

Why it happens: Performance validates early buyers, stories spread, and non-professional investors decide to join. Many latecomers enter due to FOMO rather than fundamental reassessment.

Who participates: Retail investors, mainstream funds, financial media, influencers.

Common signals:

- Rapid increase in search interest, social mentions, and news coverage.
- Flow into related ETFs or instruments.
- Reduced volatility on up moves, but more participation on rallies.

- Beginner traders and new account openings focused on the asset class.

Practical action:

- Begin trimming small portions to realize gains, especially if valuation is moving away from conservative fair value.
- Reassess risk: widen your mental model from "this single idea" to "crowd-driven speculation."
- Protect profits with partial sells and tighter stops on remaining holdings.

5. Euphoria Peak (HIGH Zone)

What it is: The emotional apex: prices are parabolic, narratives dominate, and skepticism is marginalized. Liquidity is abundant on the way up; downside becomes rare in sentiment.

Why it happens: Stories of disruption, "new paradigm" thinking, and easy money combine with momentum to create runaway rallies. Retail leverage often peaks here.

Who participates: Late-stage retail, leveraged speculators, media-driven buyers; by contrast, insiders and smart institutions may begin to quietly sell.

Common signals:

- Parabolic charts and vertical price moves.
- Headlines proclaiming inevitability ("the next X").
- Massive inflows and high retail engagement metrics.
- Insider selling and institutional distribution despite rising prices.

Practical action:

- Execute structured scale-outs: lock in profits, reduce exposure, and reallocate to lower-risk areas.
- Implement protective measures (tighten stops, convert part to cash or hedges).
- Avoid fresh large purchases driven by fear of missing out.

6. Distribution

What it is: A phase where smart money and early investors quietly sell into demand. Price may hold or drift, but the underlying balance shifts: supply builds while demand thins.

Why it happens: Those who bought earlier realize their gains and take liquidity as new buyers imagine upside remains. Distribution is often masked as normal trading days.

Who participates: Institutions taking profits, insiders cashing out, sophisticated funds reducing net exposure.

Common signals:

- Increased selling in the face of small news or without news.
- Rising supply-of-lots being offered; block trades near highs.
- Divergences between price and momentum indicators.
- Volume patterns showing high-volume down-days or distribution bars.

Practical action:

- Continue to reduce positions according to your exit plan.
- Watch for weakening internals (breadth, volume on up-days).
- Avoid re-entering until a true reset or value-based opportunity appears.

7. Panic Crash

What it is: Rapid reversal: prices fall sharply as sentiment flips. Forced selling, margin calls, and cascade effects amplify declines. What was once liquidity on the way up becomes illiquidity on the way down.

Why it happens: A catalyst (news, macro shift, liquidity shock) removes confidence; momentum reverses and sellers overwhelm buyers. Leverage and automated selling can accelerate declines.

Who participates: Panicked retail, forced sellers (margin calls, redemptions), short sellers, opportunistic buyers at the tail end.

Common signals:

- Large, fast down-candles with very high volume.
- Volatility spiking and liquidity evaporating.
- Newsflow shifting from positive to panic-driven narratives.
- Fear indicators at extreme levels.

Practical action:

- Protect capital first: honor stop-losses or hedges you set earlier.
- Avoid emotional selling—follow your pre-defined crisis rules.
- If you kept dry powder and fundamentals remain intact for certain assets, begin watching for accumulation signals (this is where the next cycle's LOW zones will form).

8. Reset → Accumulation

What it is: The market finds a new equilibrium. Prices stabilize, fundamentals reassert themselves, and fear becomes dominant again. The cycle returns to accumulation as long-term buyers begin the process anew.

Why it happens: After panic, clarity returns: survivors reassess value, credit conditions settle, and the market digests the shock. Slowly, the fear-driven discount unwinds and selective buyers re-enter.

Who participates: Long-term investors, contrarians, patient institutions, and opportunistic private capital.

Common signals:

- Volatility eases and price stops making new lows.
- Early signs of fundamental stabilization (earnings troughing, demand normalizing).
- Reduced headline panic; pessimism peaks then gradually lessens.
- Insider or institutional accumulation may begin again.

Practical action:

- Re-deploy capital slowly using the Low Zone checklist and your scale-in rules.
- Reevaluate the long-term thesis with conservative assumptions.
- Keep discipline: accumulation is slow, not dramatic — the best opportunities are often quiet.

Putting the Cycle Together — The Rule

The Market Cycle Map simplifies a complex truth into a usable rule:

Buy in fear-heavy early phases.
Sell in greed-heavy late phases.

This rule is simple in words and difficult in practice because it asks you to do the opposite of the crowd. The real power lies in using objective signals from each phase — valuation, volume, sentiment, insider activity, and price structure — to turn a psychological contrarian stance into a repeatable, disciplined strategy.

Practical Summary

- Map any asset to a phase before acting. Ask: *Is this accumulation, momentum, public participation, or euphoria?*
- Use different playbooks for each phase: accumulation = buy/scale; momentum = manage and protect; public participation = trim; euphoria = sell; distribution = exit; panic = protect; reset = prepare.
- Preserve capital and optionality through strict sizing and staged entries/exits.
- Remember: cycles repeat but do not look identical — the signals are similar and the psychology is the same.

The Rule Buy in fear-heavy early phases. Sell in greed-heavy late phases.

3.2 Deep Psychological Breakdown of Each Phase

Understanding market tops requires more than charts or valuations — it requires understanding people. Peaks are not created by fundamentals; they are created by behavior.

Every market top goes through a predictable psychological sequence. Different types of investors enter and exit at different stages, the media changes tone accordingly, and institutions behave in specific, repeatable ways.

This section breaks down each phase of a typical HIGH-zone cycle through five lenses:

- Who buys?
- Who sells?
- What the media says?
- How social sentiment behaves?
- What institutions quietly do?

1. Early Euphoria Phase

Who Buys:

- Smart retail investors who spotted early momentum.
- Momentum traders.
- Hedge funds betting on trend continuation.

Who Sells:

- Almost no one. Everyone believes the rally is "just getting started."

Media Tone:

- Increasingly positive.
- Feature stories about strong earnings or innovation.
- Analysts begin raising targets.

Social Sentiment:

- Optimistic, but not extreme.
- Conversations are analytical, discussing fundamentals.

Institutional Behavior:

- Position-building continues.
- Accumulation happens steadily.

At this stage, the rally still has grounding in fundamentals — but psychology is beginning to stretch.

2. Acceleration Phase (Momentum Turns into Mania)

Who Buys:

- Retail traders who previously ignored the asset.
- Younger investors entering due to FOMO.
- Influencer-driven buyers.

Who Sells:

- Early smart money begins trimming quietly.
- Hedge funds rotate into lower-risk assets.

Media Tone:

- Excitement increases dramatically.
- Headlines like "Record Highs" appear frequently.
- Analysts defend the rise as "justified by growth potential."

Social Sentiment:

- Loud optimism.
- People bragging about gains.
- Echo chambers forming: negative opinions dismissed.

Institutional Behavior:

- Sell pressure increases, but quietly.
- Dark pool volumes rise.

This is where emotions, not fundamentals, start driving price.

3. Peak Euphoria Phase (The HIGH Zone)

This is the most dangerous phase — the top of the top.

Who Buys:

- Last-minute retail entrants.
- New investors opening accounts to "not miss the rally."
- People with zero knowledge of the asset.
- Borrowed-money traders and gamblers.

Who Sells:

- Insiders (management, founders).
- Institutions rotating out.
- Early smart money unloading heavily.

Media Tone:

- Extreme positivity.
- Statements like "This company will redefine the future."
- Experts appear on TV to justify high valuations.
- Dissenting analysts are mocked or ignored.

Social Sentiment:

- Euphoric.
- Meme-level hype.
- Unrealistic price targets.
- "This time it's different" narratives everywhere.

Institutional Behavior:

- Aggressive selling into strength.
- Rebalancing portfolios.
- Lowering exposure quietly.

At peak euphoria, the crowd becomes overconfident — exactly when smart money exits.

4. Distribution Phase (The Top Is Formed)

Who Buys:

- Late-phase retail investors who fear missing out.
- People buying because of headlines, not fundamentals.

Who Sells:

- Institutions — systematically.
- Insiders through planned selling windows.
- Early trend followers who see warning signs.

Media Tone:

- Still optimistic.
- Analysts continue raising targets.
- "Breakout" coverage pushes more retail buyers in.

Social Sentiment:

- Overconfident.
- Hype communities strongest at this stage.
- Criticism dismissed as "FUD."

Institutional Behavior:

- Large-volume selling disguised inside bullish days.
- Hedge funds hedging positions with options.

Distribution is the silent climax — the peak formed not by buying, but by the shift from accumulation to disposal.

5. The First Crack (Beginnings of Decline)

Who Buys:

- Dip-buyers who believe the rally is still intact.
- High-conviction retail traders.

Who Sells:

- Institutions accelerate selling.
- Momentum traders exiting positions.

Media Tone:

- "Healthy correction."
- "Great buying opportunity."
- Justifications for why the trend is still alive.

Social Sentiment:

- Mixed — confident but defensive.
- Blame placed on temporary news or external events.

Institutional Behavior:

- Selling becomes more transparent.
- Volatility rises despite attempts to maintain optimism.

This is often the last chance to exit near the top.

6. Downtrend and Capitulation

Who Buys:

- Almost no one.
- Only disciplined contrarians begin watching, not buying.

Who Sells:

- Retail panic sellers.
- Late entrants losing 40–70%.
- Over-leveraged traders forced out.

Media Tone:

- Extremely negative.

- Headlines full of fear, blame, and crisis.
- Analysts downgrade aggressively.

Social Sentiment:

- Fear, anger, and despair.
- Communities collapse.
- Narratives flip: from "to the moon" → "it was a scam."

Institutional Behavior:

- Institutions have already exited.
- Some long-term funds begin quietly preparing to accumulate.

This final stage ends the HIGH cycle — and sets the stage for a future LOW zone.

Summary

Across all phases, the psychological pattern repeats:

Early smart money enters first. Late emotional money enters last — and exits first.

Understanding this psychological choreography allows you to identify HIGH zones with clarity, avoid dangerous tops, and execute Sell High with confidence and discipline.

3.3 Historical Cycle Comparisons

Every market cycle is unique in its headlines but identical in its underlying human behavior. To understand Buy Low–Sell High at a deeper level, it helps to examine multiple historical cycles and see how fear, recovery, momentum, euphoria, and correction unfold in different eras.

This section compares three major cycles of the modern Indian and global markets. Each cycle highlights the same repeating pattern:

Fear → Accumulation → Recovery → Momentum → Euphoria → Correction → Reset

1. The 2008–2013 Cycle: From Global Collapse to Multi-Year Revival

The 2008 financial crisis remains one of the most dramatic LOW zones in modern history. Markets globally fell 50–70%, triggered by the collapse of Lehman Brothers, the mortgage bubble, and systemic financial panic.

2008–2009: The LOW Zone

Fear dominated:

- Banks failed.
- Global credit froze.
- Headlines predicted "end of the financial system."
- Stocks everywhere traded at 10–20 year lows.

Valuations collapsed:

- Blue-chip Indian stocks fell 50–75%.
- Global indices reached historic discounts.
- Sentiment hit maximum pessimism.

But fundamentals slowly stabilized:

- Policy support from central banks.
- Liquidity injections globally.
- Banks recapitalized.

This was one of the clearest LOW zones of the century.

2010–2012: The Recovery + Momentum Phase

Markets rebounded powerfully:

- Nifty bounced from 2,500 → 6,000.
- U.S. markets began decade-long bull run.

Investor psychology shifted:

- Fear → cautious optimism.
- Cautious optimism → confidence.

Fundamentals strengthened:

- Earnings normalized.
- Credit markets reopened.
- High-quality companies led the charge.

2013: Mini-Euphoria + Reset

Signs of excess:

- Retail participation surged.
- High-beta stocks soared.
- Analysts raised targets aggressively.

What followed: A healthy global correction driven by U.S. tapering fears, resetting valuations and clearing excess.

This cycle reinforced a timeless truth: **The best long-term returns are captured by entering in deep fear and holding through multi-year recoveries.**

—

2. The 2015–2017 Cycle: Earnings Recovery and the Midcap Mania

This cycle shows how optimism can grow gradually — and then explode suddenly.

2015: The Build-Up

Valuations reasonable:

- Nifty valuations were fair.
- Midcaps recovering from 2013 corrections.

Macro tailwinds:

- Lower inflation.
- Policy stability.
- Corporate earnings bottoming out.

Sentiment was optimistic, but not euphoric.

2016: Early Momentum

Price action strengthened:

- Midcaps and smallcaps began outperforming.
- Domestic inflows surged into equity funds.

Retail participation increased:

- New DIIs became structural buyers (SIPs rising).

2017: The Euphoria Peak (A High-Zone Masterpiece)

This was one of India's biggest midcap HIGH zones ever.

Clear HIGH-zone signals:

- Midcaps up 100–300% in a year.
- Every stock became a "multibagger story."
- Social media flooded with unrealistic projections.
- Valuations exceeded long-term averages massively.
- Retail sentiment hyper-bullish.
- Huge mutual fund inflows to midcap & smallcap funds.

Outcome:

- 2018–2019 crash hit midcaps hard.
- Many stocks fell 50–80%.

This cycle showed that **midcaps amplify both ends of the cycle — fear and euphoria.**

—

3. The 2020–2023 Cycle: Pandemic Panic to Liquidity-Driven Supercycle

This is the most recent and emotionally extreme cycle of modern history.

2020: Global Panic — One of the Fastest LOW Zones Ever

Fear hit maximum levels:

- Markets fell 35–60% in weeks.
- Lockdowns triggered economic paralysis.
- Media predicted depression-like scenarios.

Assets became massively undervalued:

- Blue-chip stocks at decade-low valuations.
- Global real estate panic.
- Bitcoin crashed to $3,800.

This was a perfect technical + psychological LOW zone: **temporary shock + intact long-term fundamentals.**

2021: Momentum → Euphoria Across Asset Classes

Record liquidity + stimulus:

- Central banks injected trillions.
- Retail participation exploded.
- Zero-interest-rate environment triggered risk-on frenzy.

Clear HIGH-zone developments:

- Tesla and megacap tech soared.
- Bitcoin surged to $69,000.
- Meme stocks exploded (GME, AMC).
- Indian midcaps and smallcaps rallied sharply.
- Social media hype reached extremes.

This was one of the strongest global HIGH zones in decades.

2022–2023: Reset + Normalization

Corrections across the board:

- Bitcoin fell 75%.
- Tech stocks corrected 40–70%.
- Global tightening reversed liquidity excess.

Investors learned again: Euphoria cycles always end in cooling.
—

Summary

Across 2008–2013, 2015–2017, and 2020–2023, one pattern holds:

Fear creates LOW zones. Euphoria creates HIGH zones. Cycles repeat forever.

Different catalysts. Different narratives. Same psychological and valuation structure.

These historical comparisons help you recognize where we are in any cycle — and apply Buy Low–Sell High with clarity and discipline.

Key Takeaways

- **Markets move in predictable emotional and structural cycles.** Every asset passes through phases of fear, recovery, momentum, euphoria, collapse, and reset. These patterns repeat because human behavior repeats.
- **The cycle has eight essential stages:** Accumulation → Early Uptick → Momentum → Public Participation → Euphoria Peak → Distribution → Panic Crash → Reset → back to Accumulation.
- **LOW zones appear in fear-heavy early phases.** Accumulation and Early Uptick offer the best opportunities because price trades below value, fundamentals stabilize, and smart money accumulates.
- **HIGH zones appear in greed-heavy late phases.** Public Participation, Euphoria, and Distribution are where risk becomes asymmetric, valuations stretch, sentiment overheats, and insiders exit.
- **Fear compresses price below value; greed inflates price above value.** Recognizing these distortions allows you to act rationally when others act emotionally.
- **Accumulation is quiet; euphoria is loud.** The best opportunities rarely announce themselves. The worst risks often dominate headlines and social media.
- **Momentum and Public Participation are transition phases.** They bridge undervaluation to overvaluation, and create both tactical opportunities and early warning signals.
- **Distribution hides beneath the surface.** Price may appear strong, but smart money is reducing exposure while retail investors enter late.
- **Panic crashes are not the end—they are resets.** Forced selling drives price far below value, setting up the next accumulation phase and the next opportunity cycle.
- **The timeless rule:**

  Buy in fear-heavy early phases. Sell in greed-heavy late phases.

  This rule aligns behavior with value, not emotion.
- **Mapping any asset onto the cycle gives you clarity.** Instead of guessing, you can diagnose the phase, understand the psychology behind the price, and act with discipline.

With this cycle map in hand, you can now combine valuation, sentiment, fundamentals, and psychology into a complete Buy Low–Sell High strategy. The next chapter builds the full BL–SH System and turns these patterns into precise execution rules.

Chapter 4

The Psychology Engine

Markets do not beat investors — their own minds do. Every bad entry, every panic exit, every missed opportunity, every painful loss can be traced back to a predictable psychological bias. The rule "Buy Low, Sell High" is simple, but human behavior makes it incredibly hard to follow.

Fear pushes people to sell at the bottom. Greed pushes them to buy at the top. The crowd amplifies both.

This chapter exposes the psychological forces that sabotage rational decisions — loss aversion, recency bias, FOMO, herd instinct, anchoring, and overconfidence. These instincts evolved for survival, not for financial markets, and they cause predictable, repeatable mistakes across every cycle.

More importantly, this chapter shows how to fix them.

By using pre-defined rules, structured systems, checklists, and planning before action, you can override emotion with discipline. You will learn how to build a psychological engine that supports intelligent behavior instead of fighting it — turning mental weakness into a durable competitive advantage.

This chapter is where emotional discipline begins.

4.1 Why People Violate Buy Low–Sell High

The rule *Buy Low–Sell High* is simple. Yet most investors consistently do the opposite. They buy after large rallies and sell after large declines. This is not because they lack intelligence or information — it is because human psychology is wired in ways that conflict directly with rational investing.

Below are the core psychological forces that repeatedly push people away from intelligent decisions and into predictable, destructive behavior.

1. Loss Aversion: The Pain of Losing Is Twice as Strong as the Pleasure of Winning

Loss aversion is one of the most powerful and universal human biases. A small loss often feels more painful than an equivalent gain feels good. This imbalance drives investors to act emotionally:

- They sell during declines to "stop the pain," even when value is intact.
- They refuse to buy during fear because they fear losing more.
- They hold losers too long, hoping the loss will disappear.

Loss aversion is why investors sell low in panic instead of buying low with logic. It turns temporary volatility into permanent mistakes.

2. Recency Bias: Believing the Last Few Months Will Continue Forever

Recency bias convinces people that recent price action defines the future:

- After a crash, they believe prices will keep falling indefinitely.
- After a rally, they believe the rise will never end.

This bias makes investors:

- distrust early bottoms,
- chase late-stage tops,
- confuse short-term noise with long-term direction.

Recency bias creates emotional blindness. It convinces people that today's trend is permanent, even when it's not.

3. Fear of Missing Out (FOMO): The Desire Not to Be Left Behind

FOMO is the emotional engine of manias. When an asset moves sharply upward, people experience a powerful social and psychological pressure to participate:

- "Everyone else is making money."
- "I'll regret it if I don't buy now."
- "This is my chance — I need to act."

FOMO leads to:

- buying assets after large rallies,
- ignoring valuation completely,
- taking oversized, reckless positions,
- entering exactly when smart money is exiting.

FOMO turns the late stages of the cycle into emotional traps.

4. Herd Instinct: Trusting the Crowd Over Independent Thinking

Humans evolved in groups — and our brains still believe that safety lies in numbers. In markets, this instinct becomes harmful.

Herd behavior makes investors:

- buy because others are buying,
- sell because others are selling,
- trust the crowd even when fundamentals disagree,
- confuse popularity with correctness.

The herd buys in euphoria and sells in panic — precisely the opposite of the Buy Low–Sell High principle.

5. Anchoring: Fixating on Old Prices and Irrelevant Reference Points

Anchoring occurs when investors latch onto a specific price and use it as a mental anchor:

- "It used to be $100, so $80 must be cheap."
- "It's never been above $200, so it can't go higher."
- "It fell from $60 to $20 — it must rebound."

Anchoring prevents rational valuation analysis. It causes investors to:

- buy assets that have fallen (even if value has collapsed),
- refuse to buy assets that have risen (even if fundamentals justify it),
- ignore what the asset is truly worth today.

Anchoring ties decisions to irrelevant numbers instead of objective value.

6. Overconfidence: Mistaking Luck for Skill

Overconfidence makes investors believe they understand markets better than they do. A few early wins can create a dangerous illusion:

- they take larger positions than their risk capacity,
- they ignore warning signals,
- they underestimate downside probabilities,
- they believe they can time tops and bottoms perfectly.

Overconfidence pushes investors to hold too long in euphoric phases and to buy aggressively during manias — exactly when the risk is greatest.

Why These Biases Matter

These six psychological forces combine into a predictable and destructive loop:

Fear → Selling Low → Regret → FOMO → Buying High → Loss → Fear

This loop is the enemy of wealth. It is why markets create mispricing, why cycles exist, and why individuals underperform their own assets.

Understanding these biases is the first step. The next step is replacing emotion with structure — the focus of the next section.

4.2 How to Fix Psychology

Psychology cannot be removed from investing — but it can be outpowered. The most successful investors do not rely on emotional strength. They rely on structure. They build systems that override instinct and turn discipline into something automatic.

Below are the four core mechanisms that transform psychology from a liability into a competitive advantage.

1. Pre-Defined Rules: Decide Before You Act

The worst time to make a decision is during volatility. When prices move fast, the emotional brain takes over and the rational brain goes offline. The antidote is **pre-defined rules**: clear decisions made when you are calm, logical, and objective.

Examples of powerful pre-defined rules:

- "I buy only when valuation is 20–50% below fair value."
- "I sell 25–50% of my position if price becomes parabolic."

- "I cut risk if fundamentals change materially."
- "I do not add to losing positions unless value improves."
- "I size positions based on volatility, not emotion."

Pre-defined rules remove guesswork. They eliminate emotional improvisation. They convert chaos into disciplined execution.

The key principle: Decide the rule when you are calm. Execute the rule when the market is emotional.

2. System ¿ Emotion: Build a Process That Runs Automatically

A system is a structured way of thinking. It defines how you evaluate assets, how you enter, how you exit, and how you size positions. When you follow a system, your decisions become consistent and repeatable.

Why systems outperform emotions:

- emotions change minute to minute — systems stay constant,
- emotions follow price — systems follow logic,
- emotions react — systems anticipate,
- emotions isolate events — systems see cycles.

A robust investing system includes:

1. clear valuation framework (what is "low," what is "high"),
2. entry rules (when value ¿ price),
3. exit rules (when price ¿ value),
4. risk rules (position size + diversification),
5. behavior rules (no impulsive decisions).

The stronger your system, the less power your emotions have.

3. Checklists: Prevent Mistakes Before They Happen

Even experienced investors slip when markets move quickly. A checklist acts as a barrier between you and your mistakes. It forces you to verify what matters before you act.

A strong checklist includes:

- valuation confirmation ("Is this truly undervalued or overvalued?"),
- fundamental health check ("Are the core drivers intact?"),

- sentiment reading ("Is this fear-driven or greed-driven?"),
- risk evaluation ("Can I hold this if it drops 20–30%?"),
- time-horizon alignment ("Does this match my goals?"),
- capital allocation check ("Am I sizing rationally?").

Checklists save you from:

- buying too late,
- selling too early,
- chasing hype,
- holding through euphoria,
- panicking in downturns,
- acting without clarity.

A checklist slows you down just enough to avoid emotional errors. It trades impulse for intention.

4. Planning Before Action: Prepare for Volatility Before It Arrives

Most emotional mistakes happen because investors are unprepared. They react to volatility instead of planning for it. The solution is to decide your responses before the event happens.

Planning before action includes:

- defining what you will do during a 20–40% crash,
- deciding how you will scale in during a LOW zone,
- outlining your exit strategy for a HIGH zone,
- setting alerts for key price levels and fundamentals,
- rehearsing scenarios ("If X happens, I will do Y").

This preparation turns fear into readiness and surprises into opportunities.

Benefits of planning:

- you never panic sell,
- you never FOMO buy,
- you avoid hesitation during LOW zones,

- you avoid greed during HIGH zones,
- your behavior becomes consistent across cycles.

Planning makes your future self predictable. It replaces panic with execution.

Psychology Is Fixed by Architecture, Not Willpower

Most investors try to "control their emotions." This almost always fails.

The right approach is to build a psychological architecture that limits emotional influence:

- rules make decisions automatic,
- systems make behavior consistent,
- checklists reduce impulsiveness,
- planning prevents panic.

This is how psychology becomes an advantage instead of a weakness.

You don't rise to the level of your intentions. You fall to the level of your systems.

The next section builds on this foundation and gives you the tools to stay disciplined across all market conditions.

4.3 Behavioral Tools and Exercises

Markets don't beat investors — investors beat themselves.

To master Buy Low–Sell High, you must first master your own psychology. This section gives you a set of practical, repeatable behavioral tools and exercises designed to break emotional impulses, strengthen discipline, and create internal systems that prevent you from violating the BL–SH rules.

These tools are simple to learn, easy to apply, and powerful enough to reshape your behavior across every market cycle.

1. The Emotional-Scorecard Method

Your emotions dictate your timing. The Emotional-Scorecard method forces you to convert feelings into measurable signals.

How It Works:

Before every buy or sell, rate your emotional state on a scale of 1–10:

- 1–3 = Fear, anxiety, hesitation
- 4–6 = Neutral, calm, analytical

- 7–10 = Excitement, greed, FOMO

Interpretation:

- If you score yourself **7–10**, you should NOT buy. High excitement = high risk of buying near a top.
- If you score **1–3**, you should NOT sell. High fear = high risk of selling near a bottom.

Why It Works: It separates emotional impulses from rational decisions. Your score becomes a protective brake before mistakes.

2. The Panic-Proof Checklist

During market crashes, emotions overwhelm logic. This checklist ensures you freeze your reactions and assess reality correctly.

Before selling anything in a panic, ask:

1. Has the business fundamentally changed?
2. Is this a temporary macro shock?
3. Is valuation now cheap relative to history?
4. Are institutions accumulating?
5. Are headlines more emotional than factual?
6. Is my fear driven by price movement, not fundamentals?
7. Would I buy this asset at this valuation if I didn't already own it?

If the answer to most questions is **"fundamentals still intact"**, you should HOLD or BUY — not panic sell.

Purpose: To prevent catastrophic emotional exits during LOW zones.

3. Decision Journal Template

Your brain forgets mistakes, but markets do not. A decision journal exposes your patterns, biases, and emotional triggers.

Template:

- **Date:**
- **Decision:** Buy / Sell / Hold
- **Reason:** (Fundamental? Technical? Emotional?)
- **Emotional Score (1–10):**

- **LOW/HIGH Zone Check:**
  - Is price undervalued or overvalued?
  - Is sentiment fearful or euphoric?
  - Is this decision driven by panic or FOMO?
- **Expected Outcome:**
- **Alternative Options Considered:**
- **Post-Result Reflection (filled later):**

Why It Works:

- Makes your thinking visible.
- Reveals emotional patterns.
- Holds you accountable to your system.

A decision journal is the cheapest performance coach you will ever have.

4. Loss-Aversion Training Exercise

Loss aversion is the strongest human bias. We feel the pain of a loss twice as intensely as the joy of a gain. This exercise retrains your brain to accept volatility without panic.

Exercise: "The 20% Shock Drill"

Once a month, imagine one of your holdings falling 20%. Write down:

- What would I feel?
- What would I fear?
- What action would my emotional brain push me to take?
- What action does my system tell me to take?

Then ask:

Has anything fundamental changed?

If the answer is "no," you train yourself to detach emotion from action.

Purpose: To simulate fear in a controlled, safe environment so you react rationally when real volatility hits.

5. Confirmation Bias Trap Prevention

Confirmation bias is when you only search for information that supports your view and ignore conflicting facts.

This bias causes:

- buying too late in HIGH zones,
- holding too long during euphoria,
- ignoring warnings during parabolic rallies.

Tool: The Opposing Thesis Method
Before buying or selling, force yourself to write:

"The best argument AGAINST my decision is..."

Look for:

- valuation risks,
- competitive threats,
- insider selling,
- macro/demand slowdown,
- excessive optimism in social sentiment.

If you cannot disprove your own thesis, your thinking is not complete.

Purpose: Protects you from one-sided thinking, the core driver of buying at tops.

Summary

These behavioral tools help you:

- break emotional impulses,
- reinforce rational decision-making,
- prevent buying in HIGH zones,
- prevent selling in LOW zones,
- and stay aligned with the BL–SH system.

Master the mind, and the market becomes predictable.

Key Takeaways

- **Investors fail not because of lack of knowledge, but because of psychology.** Emotional instincts—designed for survival—conflict directly with rational investing.
- **Six psychological forces drive most market mistakes:** loss aversion, recency bias, fear of missing out, herd instinct, anchoring, and overconfidence. Together, they create the predictable cycle of buying high and selling low.
- **Loss aversion causes panic selling.** The pain of losing triggers irrational exits during LOW zones, when opportunity is highest.
- **Recency bias distorts expectations.** Investors assume past weeks reflect the future, leading to chasing tops and fearing bottoms.
- **FOMO drives late-stage entries.** Emotional pressure from rising prices pulls people into markets exactly when risk is greatest.
- **Herd instinct amplifies mistakes.** Following the crowd feels safe, but the crowd buys in euphoria and sells in panic.
- **Anchoring traps investors in old price levels.** Decisions become tied to outdated numbers rather than current value.
- **Overconfidence leads to oversized, reckless trades.** A few wins convince investors they can ignore risk until they encounter a large loss.
- **Psychology cannot be controlled—only engineered.** The solution is structural, not emotional.
- **Pre-defined rules prevent emotional improvisation.** Decisions made calmly in advance outperform decisions made in fear or excitement.
- **Systems outperform instincts.** A repeatable process ensures consistent behavior across cycles.
- **Checklists eliminate avoidable mistakes.** They force verification of fundamentals, valuation, sentiment, and risk before action.
- **Planning before action prepares you for volatility.** When you know in advance how you will respond to panic and euphoria, emotions lose their power.
- **Emotional discipline is built, not born.** With the right rules, systems, and preparation, psychology becomes a competitive edge instead of a source of failure.

This chapter gives you the psychological foundation to execute the Buy Low–Sell High strategy consistently. The next chapter integrates psychology, valuation, sentiment, and cycles into your complete execution framework.

Chapter 5

The HIGH-Zone Matrix (Your Exit Model)

Knowing when to buy is only half of mastery. Knowing when to sell is the real separator.

Most investors fail not because they enter too late, but because they exit too late — holding through euphoria, ignoring danger signals, and giving back months or years of gains during sudden reversals.

The HIGH-Zone Matrix is your structured exit model. It identifies the exact conditions that appear near tops, when price is no longer supported by value, logic, or smart money. This model is the mirror image of your LOW-Zone buy framework.

The HIGH Zone forms when four forces converge:

- **Overvaluation** — price trades far above fair value.
- **Sentiment Extreme (Euphoria)** — optimism becomes delusion, fear disappears.
- **Price Acceleration** — charts go vertical, gains become unsustainably fast.
- **Smart Money Exiting** — insiders and institutions quietly sell into the crowd.

When these pillars align, upside becomes limited and downside becomes enormous. Recognizing this zone allows you to protect gains, reduce exposure, and exit before the cycle turns.

This chapter gives you a precise, evidence-based roadmap for selling high — without emotion, hesitation, or guesswork.

5.1 The 4 Pillars of the HIGH-Zone Matrix

To identify a true HIGH zone — a period where risk becomes extreme, upside becomes limited, and probability of reversal becomes high — you need a structured framework. The HIGH-Zone Matrix rests on four powerful, repeating forces that consistently appear before major peaks across stocks, crypto, commodities, real estate, indices, and even entire economic cycles.

These forces are not random. They are universal patterns rooted in valuation, human psychology, price behavior, and institutional activity.

When all four pillars align, the probability of a top becomes dramatically elevated. Each pillar signals a different dimension of excess: value, emotion, behavior, and insider intent.

Let's examine each one in depth.

1. Overvaluation: Price Detached From Fundamental Reality

Overvaluation is the foundational pillar of a HIGH zone. It occurs when price rises far beyond what the underlying asset can justify based on earnings, cash flow, assets, or long-term prospects.

Overvaluation is not a high price. It is a price unsupported by value.

Common signals of overvaluation:

- valuation multiples expand far beyond historical norms,
- price increases without corresponding growth in fundamentals,
- analysts revise targets upward based on momentum, not evidence,
- narratives replace numbers ("it's different this time"),
- DCF or intrinsic models require unrealistic assumptions to justify price,
- the asset trades at a premium to superior peers.

Overvaluation usually begins during momentum and becomes dangerous during late public participation. The deeper the disconnect, the more fragile the price becomes.

Why it matters: Overvaluation removes the fundamental floor that normally protects downside. When sentiment turns, price falls rapidly because there is no valuation support beneath it.

2. Sentiment Extreme (Euphoria): When Confidence Mutates Into Delusion

Euphoria is the psychological fuel of a market peak. It is the stage where investors stop thinking in probabilities and start believing in inevitabilities.

Euphoria changes the questions investors ask:

- from "Is this worth the price?"
- to "How high can this go?"

It changes their behavior:

- skepticism becomes rare,
- negative data is ignored,
- caution is mocked,
- investors feel certain, not unsure.

Euphoria indicators:

- media praise becomes unconditional,
- social networks flood with bullish takes and simplified charts,
- newcomers join aggressively with no understanding of risk,
- investors brag about easy gains,
- short sellers are ridiculed or disappear,
- "this time it's different" narratives dominate.

Euphoria is not about price — it's about belief. And belief is what makes late-stage markets fragile.

When sentiment becomes one-sided, all buyers have already bought, leaving no liquidity to support the price when selling begins.

3. Price Acceleration: The Parabolic Curve of Unsustainable Movement

Fundamentals normally produce gradual and steady growth. Euphoria produces vertical growth — fast, steep, and unsustainable.

Price acceleration is the chart-based pillar of a HIGH zone.

It appears when:

- price rises faster in weeks than it did in years,
- each dip is bought instantly and aggressively,
- candles elongate and become predominantly green,
- volumes explode during rallies,
- gains compress into smaller and smaller time periods.

This is the classic parabolic curve — a hallmark of mania.

Why parabolic moves collapse:

- they rely on continuous new buying at an increasing rate,
- when acceleration slows even slightly, momentum dies,
- once momentum stalls, leveraged positions unwind,
- unwinds trigger forced selling, which creates a cascade.

Price acceleration is the most visible sign of a HIGH zone. It tells you the trend is no longer supported by fundamentals or steady demand — it is supported by emotion and speed.

And speed never lasts.

4. Smart Money Exiting: Insiders and Institutions Leave Quietly

If overvaluation is the intellectual signal, and euphoria is the emotional signal, and parabolic price is the visual signal — then smart money exiting is the **behavioral confirmation.**

Smart money exits when the crowd is most excited.

This includes:

- corporate insiders selling their shares near peaks,
- institutions trimming exposure after long rallies,
- declining ownership from long-term funds,
- a rise in distribution days (sell-offs on high volume),
- large block sales executed near highs,
- lock-up expirations being fully used by insiders.

Why this signal is powerful:

- insiders know real fundamentals better than anyone,
- institutions understand cycles and crowd psychology,
- smart money sells into strength, not weakness,
- they exit gradually, leaving the peak to retail buyers.

Retail investors buy aggressively at the top. Smart money uses their enthusiasm as liquidity to sell quietly.

Why All Four Pillars Must Be Watched Together

A market peak rarely announces itself with a single warning. It signals itself through the convergence of the four pillars:

1. **Value breaks** — price outruns fundamental worth.
2. **Psychology breaks** — fear disappears, replaced by delusion.
3. **Price breaks** — the trend becomes vertical and unstable.
4. **Behavior breaks** — insiders exit while the crowd enters.

Any single pillar may appear alone. But when all four align, you are standing at or near the top of the cycle.

That is when selling becomes not just wise, but necessary to protect long-term gains and avoid catastrophic drawdowns.

How to Use the Four Pillars in Real Time

You do not need perfection. You need convergence.

If three pillars align — reduce exposure. If four pillars align — exit fully or aggressively.

The HIGH-Zone Matrix is not about prediction; it is about recognizing when risk has become asymmetric: low remaining upside, massive potential downside.

Markets peak not when price is highest, but when psychology is most extreme.

The next sections show you how to measure each pillar, how to combine them, and how to create a precise exit strategy based on the HIGH-Zone Matrix.

5.2 How to Measure the 4 Pillars

Identifying the four pillars conceptually is useful. Measuring them with precision is transformational. This section gives you clear, objective, evidence-based methods to quantify each pillar of the HIGH-Zone Matrix so you can execute exits with confidence, not emotion.

Pillar 1: How to Measure Overvaluation

Overvaluation becomes measurable when price requires increasingly unrealistic assumptions to justify itself. The goal is not to find the perfect valuation model, but to identify when value and price clearly diverge.

1. Relative Valuation Expansion

Compare valuation to:

- the asset's own historical multiples (5–10 year range),
- peers of similar quality and growth,
- market-wide averages.

Warning signs:

- P/E or EV/EBITDA is 1.5–3× historical norms,
- price-to-sales rises into double or triple digits,
- valuation exceeds superior competitors.

2. Intrinsic Value Distortion

Use DCF or cash-flow models:

- If fair value requires extreme growth (30–50% for 10 years),
- If terminal values dominate (60–80% of DCF),
- If assumptions exceed industry ceilings,

the asset is overvalued.

3. Market-Implied Expectations

When price implies:

- flawless execution,
- endless runway,
- margin expansion,
- no cyclical downturns,

then overvaluation is extreme.

4. Cross-Asset Comparisons

Compare valuation vs alternatives:

- bonds (risk-free rate),
- broader indices,
- safer sectors.

If the premium becomes unjustifiable → HIGH zone forming.

Pillar 2: How to Measure Sentiment Extreme (Euphoria)

Euphoria is psychological, but it produces clear and measurable signals.

1. Sentiment Indicators

Look for extremes in:

- investor surveys (AAII, NAAIM),
- fear/greed indices,
- volatility compression,
- skew flipping positive.

When optimism reaches historical extremes → danger.

2. Media Heat

Euphoria often shows up as:

- front-page financial news coverage,
- mainstream media segments,
- hyper-optimistic headlines,
- comparisons to previous bubbles ("the next Amazon/Bitcoin/AI boom").

3. Social Indicators

Track:

- Google Trends,
- TikTok/YouTube hype,
- influencer promotions,
- new retail accounts opening.

A spike in social visibility without parallel fundamentals → euphoria.

4. Flow Data

Massive inflows to:

- ETFs,
- meme assets,
- options volume,
- leveraged instruments.

Retail flow is loudest at tops.

Pillar 3: How to Measure Price Acceleration

Parabolic moves are quantifiable. When price rises faster than the trend can sustain, you get exponential curvature.

1. Vertical Angle of Trend

If the slope of the move:

- exceeds historical trend slope by 2–4×,
- breaks long-term resistance rapidly,
- shows price doubling or tripling in months,

the price is accelerating unsustainably.

2. Distance From Moving Averages

Measure distance from:

- 50-day MA,
- 200-day MA,
- anchored VWAP.

Danger zone:

- price 30–80% above major MAs,
- extreme RSI or MACD expansion,
- higher highs with declining momentum.

3. Candle Structure

Acceleration is visible when:

- large, consecutive green candles appear,
- dips disappear (instant buy-backs),
- volatility on declines collapses (one-sided market).

4. Volume Climax

A classic top signal:

- volume surges massively,
- then peaks,
- then price rises on lower volume.

This reflects buyer exhaustion.

Pillar 4: How to Measure Smart Money Exiting

Smart money exit signals are behavioral and highly reliable.

1. Insider Selling

Track:

- Form 4 filings,
- cluster selling (multiple insiders),
- sales near all-time highs.

Not all insider selling matters — **but patterns do.**

2. Institutional Distribution

Look for:

- reduced institutional ownership,
- large blocks sold quietly,
- distribution days (high-volume sell-offs),
- hedge funds reducing net long exposure.

3. ETF Outflows or Redemptions

When institutions redeem shares quietly at highs, it indicates they believe upside is limited.

4. Options Market Signals

Institutions often hedge before they sell:

- put buying increases,
- implied volatility rises at the top,
- skew steepens disproportionately.

5. CEO / Founder Narrative Change

Soft but powerful signals:

- leadership begins discussing "valuation premium,"
- promotional tone disappears,
- guidance becomes conservative.

These behaviors often precede exits.

Why Measurement Matters

Once you quantify the pillars, you stop guessing. You exit based on data, not emotion.

- **1 pillar** = monitor closely
- **2 pillars** = tighten stops, reduce exposure
- **3 pillars** = begin scaling out
- **4 pillars** = exit aggressively or completely

This transforms your exit strategy from reactive to proactive.

Peaks are not random. They are engineered by valuation excess, emotional excess, price excess, and insider behavior.

You now have the tools to measure all four with precision.

5.3 The HIGH-Zone Decision Worksheet

Identifying the HIGH zone requires clarity, structure, and discipline. This worksheet gives you a repeatable, 1-page system to determine whether an asset is approaching a sell zone — and how to exit with precision rather than emotion.

Use this worksheet before every major sell, trim, or scale-out decision. It includes:

- a metric scoring system,
- a red-flag checklist,
- a sentiment scale,
- and an exit-scaling map.

This worksheet transforms HIGH-zone decisions from guesswork into a structured, mechanical process.

1. Metric Scoring System (0–10 Scale)

Score each metric from 0 to 10. Higher scores indicate higher risk of a HIGH zone.

A. Valuation Stretch (0–10)

- 0–3 = Valuation normal
- 4–7 = Elevated

- 8–10 = Extreme (P/E, P/B, EV/EBITDA far above norms)

B. Price Acceleration (0–10)

- Look for parabolic moves
- Multiple weeks of +10–30% gains
- Sharp break from long-term trend lines

C. Earnings vs Price Divergence (0–10)

- Are prices rising faster than fundamentals?
- 0 = aligned, 10 = totally disconnected

D. Insider / Institutional Behavior (0–10)

- Insider selling increasing
- Funds trimming exposure
- Heavy block trades during rallies

Scoring Rule:

0–15 = Not a HIGH zone 16–25 = Caution zone — partial profit-taking 26–40 = HIGH zone — execute exits

2. Red-Flag Checklist

Tick each red flag that applies. The more boxes ticked, the closer you are to a HIGH zone.

Valuation Red Flags

- P/E above long-term sector average
- Market cap rising faster than revenue
- Analysts raising targets aggressively

Price Action Red Flags

- Parabolic chart pattern
- Multiple large green candles with no pullback
- Gap-up openings and runaway rallies

Narrative Red Flags

- "This time it's different"
- "Valuation doesn't matter now"

- Stories of dominance, monopoly, or infinite growth

Behavioral Red Flags

- New investors rushing in
- Social media hype exploding
- Emotional, not fundamental, buying

Institutional Red Flags

- Insider selling
- Mutual funds trimming
- High block-deal activity

Rule: If 7 or more red flags are checked → high probability of a top.

3. Sentiment Scale (Fear–Neutral–Euphoria)

Use this scale to assess crowd psychology:

Fear (1–3)	Neutral (4–6)	Euphoria (7–10)
Negative headlines	Balanced coverage	Headlines everywhere
Retail absent	Calm tone	New investors entering
Influencers quiet	Mixed opinions	Extreme hype & targets
"Be cautious" sentiment	Normal volatility	"Go all in" sentiment

Interpretation:

- **1–3** → Safe zone
- **4–6** → Watch carefully
- **7–10** → HIGH zone: begin exit strategy

4. Exit Scaling Map (How to Sell in the HIGH Zone)

This provides a structured, multi-step exit plan so you don't dump or panic-sell.

Step 1: Initial Trim — 25%

- Triggered when valuation hits fair-value ceiling
- Or when sentiment scale crosses 7+

Step 2: Secondary Trim — 25%

- Triggered by clear HIGH-zone signs: parabolic moves, mass retail influx

- Protects profits and reduces exposure

Step 3: Trailing Stop — Remaining 50%

- Set a dynamic stop-loss below the fast-moving trend
- Allows upside but limits downside
- Lets winners run while locking in gains

Step 4: Full Exit (If Triggered)

- Price breaks trailing stop
- Narrative collapses
- Volume spikes with selling pressure

5. How to Use This Worksheet

Before every sell decision:

1. Score all four metrics.
2. Tick all relevant red flags.
3. Check your sentiment scale number.
4. Follow the exit map exactly.

If metrics + sentiment + red flags align → execute exits without hesitation.

This worksheet removes emotion from selling — and replaces it with structure, logic, and consistency.

Key Takeaways

- **Selling well is as important as buying well.** Most investors lose money not by entering wrong, but by exiting late — holding through euphoria and ignoring danger signals.
- **The HIGH Zone is a condition, not a price level.** A price becomes dangerous only when value, psychology, behavior, and price action all detach from fundamentals.
- **The HIGH-Zone Matrix has four pillars:**
    1. **Overvaluation** — price trades far above fair value.

2. **Sentiment Extreme (Euphoria)** — optimism becomes delusion.
3. **Price Acceleration** — charts turn parabolic and unsustainable.
4. **Smart Money Exiting** — insiders and institutions quietly sell.

- **Overvaluation removes the fundamental safety net.** When price outruns value, downside risk becomes large and sudden.
- **Euphoria is the psychological peak of the cycle.** Skepticism disappears, narratives dominate, and retail investors flood in late.
- **Parabolic price acceleration is the visual fingerprint of tops.** Fast, vertical moves rely on constant new demand — once momentum slows, reversals turn violent.
- **Smart money exits when the crowd is most excited.** Insiders, institutions, and long-term funds sell into strength, using late retail enthusiasm as liquidity.
- **The convergence of pillars is the danger signal.** One pillar = monitor. Two pillars = reduce exposure. Three pillars = start scaling out. Four pillars = exit aggressively.
- **The HIGH-Zone Matrix transforms selling into a system.** You no longer guess tops or react emotionally — you follow objective signals rooted in valuation, psychology, price behavior, and smart-money activity.
- **Exiting is not prediction — it is probability.** When all four pillars align, remaining upside is small and potential downside is enormous.

This chapter gives you the tools to sell high with discipline. The next chapter integrates both LOW-Zone and HIGH-Zone frameworks into your complete Buy Low–Sell High execution system.

Chapter 6

The BL–SH SYSTEM: The 7-Step Method

The Buy Low–Sell High principle only becomes powerful when it is transformed into a system. Without structure, investors fall into emotion, randomness, and guesswork. With structure, every decision follows logic, evidence, and repeatable rules.

The BL–SH System is your complete, end-to-end methodology for identifying undervalued assets, entering at the right moment, exiting at the right moment, and repeating the cycle for long-term compounding.

It is simple, practical, and designed to work across stocks, crypto, commodities, indices, and real estate — any cyclical asset.

This chapter introduces the 7-step method that forms the backbone of this entire book: a clear framework for scanning, valuing, buying, exiting, and compounding with discipline instead of emotion.

6.1 Step 1 — Scan for Undervalued Assets

Finding great opportunities begins with identifying assets that are trading below their true worth. This step is not about prediction. It is not about guessing what will rise next. It is about systematically scanning the entire market to locate assets that are already priced at a discount — assets where the downside is limited and the upside is asymmetrically large.

A disciplined scan gives you your opportunity pool. Without it, everything else in the BL–SH System becomes guesswork.

To scan effectively, you use a combination of valuation tools, fundamental screens, and sentiment indicators that help flag potential LOW-zone candidates. These tools do not replace judgment — they filter and focus it.

Below are the core components of a world-class scanning process.

1. Valuation Tools: Identifying Genuine Price–Value Gaps

Valuation tools help you identify assets that are priced cheaply relative to earnings, assets, or cash flow. You do not need complex models here — simplicity is powerful and scalable.

a. Price-to-Earnings (P/E)

- Compares current price to current earnings.
- Lower P/E can indicate undervaluation *if* earnings quality is stable.
- Compare versus: — the company's historical average, — industry averages, — peers of similar quality.

Buy signal: P/E significantly below historical norms + stable or improving earnings.

b. Price-to-Book (P/B)

- Useful for asset-heavy sectors: banks, real estate, energy, infrastructure, manufacturing.
- A P/B under 1.0 often signals the market is pricing the company below the value of its assets.

Buy signal: P/B ¡ 1.0 with strong balance sheet and no structural issues.

c. Free Cash Flow Yield (FCF Yield)

This is one of the most powerful valuation metrics.

- FCF yield = Free Cash Flow / Market Cap.
- A high FCF yield indicates the business is producing significant cash relative to its price.

Buy signal: FCF yield significantly higher than the market average or its own historical norm.

2. Sentiment Tools: Identifying Fear-Based Mispricing

Often, undervaluation is created not by fundamentals but by emotion. This is where sentiment-based tools such as RSI and volatility indices become essential.

a. Relative Strength Index (RSI)

- Measures how overbought or oversold an asset is.
- RSI ¡ 30 often signals fear-driven selling.
- RSI ¡ 20 signals extreme fear or capitulation.

Buy signal: Deep oversold RSI + stable fundamentals.

b. Volatility Indices (VIX, VXN, sector-specific fear indicators)

Volatility spikes often occur during panic selling.

- High volatility = fear.
- Fear often pushes price below fair value.
- VIX spikes correlate with LOW-zone setups.

Buy signal: Volatility surges while fundamentals remain unchanged.

3. Relative Scans: Searching for the Cheapest Among Peers

A powerful way to identify undervalued assets is to compare them against similar assets.

Compare:

- valuation multiples,
- growth rates,
- margins,
- capital structure,
- historical ranges.

If a fundamentally strong asset is significantly cheaper than similar companies, you may be looking at a mispricing.

4. Macro and Sector Screens: Look for Entire Groups Mispriced

Markets often misprice entire sectors due to:

- macro fear,
- temporary regulatory shocks,
- recession risk,

- interest-rate anxiety,
- geopolitical events.

Scanning by sector helps you catch opportunities created by broad panic rather than company-specific problems.

5. Combine Tools for High-Probability Candidates

One metric alone is not enough. The magic happens when multiple undervaluation signals align:

Low P/E + High FCF + RSI Oversold + Volatility Spike = Strong LOW-Zone Candidate

This is the type of alignment you want before moving to Step 2.

Why This Step Matters

The BL–SH System starts with a high-quality scan because:

- You avoid chasing hype.
- You let value guide you, not narratives.
- You create a pool of opportunities that the market is temporarily mispricing.
- You eliminate 90% of noise and focus only on asymmetric setups.

Scanning is not about predicting the future. It is about identifying assets where the present offers an exceptional risk–reward profile.

You cannot Buy Low unless you first find low. Step 1 gives you the map.

6.2 Step 2 — Validate Fundamentals

Scanning helps you find assets that *look* cheap. Validating fundamentals tells you whether they *deserve* to be cheap — or whether the market is mispricing a fundamentally strong asset.

This step separates value opportunities from value traps.

A low price means nothing unless the underlying engine of the business (or asset) remains strong, durable, and capable of long-term cash generation. Fundamentals are the foundation beneath price. If the foundation is cracked, a discount is justified — and dangerous.

Validating fundamentals means examining four critical pillars: **revenue, debt, cash flow, moat**. Together, they reveal the true health, resilience, and longevity of an asset.

1. Revenue: Stability, Growth, and Quality

Revenue is the lifeblood of a business. It tells you whether the company is generating demand, maintaining market presence, and sustaining economic relevance.

a. Revenue Trend

Look for:

- stable or rising revenue,
- small declines that are temporary or cyclical,
- avoidance of large, persistent multi-year declines.

Red flags:

- multi-year shrinking revenue,
- loss of major customers,
- structural disruptions (technology replacing the product).

b. Revenue Quality

Not all revenue is equal.

High-quality revenue includes:

- recurring revenue (subscriptions, contracts),
- diversified customer base,
- steady demand,
- pricing power.

c. Revenue vs. Price

If revenue is healthy but price collapsed, this is often a sign of mispricing — a LOW-zone candidate.

2. Debt: Stability, Safety, and Survival

Debt determines survivability during downturns. Even a great business can collapse under excessive leverage.

a. Debt-to-Equity and Leverage Ratios

Compare leverage to:

- historical levels of the company,
- industry averages,
- free cash flow generation capability.

Red flag: Debt growing faster than revenue or cash flow.

b. Interest Coverage

Check whether operating income or cash flow can comfortably pay interest.

- Coverage ratio ¿ 3 is healthy.
- Coverage ratio ¡ 1.5 increases risk dramatically.

c. Debt Maturity Profile

A silent but critical detail:

- Is major debt coming due soon?
- Does the company have enough liquidity to refinance?

Debt is not bad — unmanageable debt is.

3. Cash Flow: The Real Proof of Strength

Earnings can be manipulated. Cash flow cannot.
Cash flow validates whether the business truly generates money.

a. Free Cash Flow (FCF)

Look for:

- consistent positive FCF,
- rising FCF over time,
- temporary dips explained by investment rather than deterioration.

b. Cash Conversion

Healthy businesses convert earnings into cash at reasonable rates. If cash lags far behind earnings, investigate why.

c. Cash Reserves

Large cash reserves give the company:

- resilience in downturns,
- ability to invest during crises,
- ability to survive temporary negative sentiment.

Cash flow strength is one of the most powerful buffers during panic periods.

4. Moat: Competitive Advantage and Durability

The moat is the most important long-term fundamental. It tells you whether the company can defend its market position and maintain pricing power over time.

Types of strong moats:

- brand dominance,
- network effects,
- cost advantages,
- intellectual property,
- high switching costs,
- regulatory barriers,
- unique distribution,
- supply chain control.

Why moats matter: A business with a moat rebounds faster, survives downturns better, and compounds value across cycles.

How These Four Pillars Work Together

Validating fundamentals is not about perfection — it's about identifying *durability*.

The ideal LOW-zone candidate has:

- stable or improving revenue,
- manageable debt,
- strong free cash flow,
- a defensible moat,

combined with:

- temporary fear,
- emotional selling,
- price dislocation.

This combination creates asymmetric opportunity — the heart of Buy Low–Sell High.

The Purpose of Step 2

Validating fundamentals answers one crucial question:

"Is this truly undervalued — or is it cheap for a reason?"

Fundamentals protect you from value traps. They let you buy low with conviction because you know the business beneath the price is strong.

Only once fundamentals are validated do you move to Step 3: **Estimating fair value.**

6.3 Step 3 — Estimate Fair Value

Once you identify undervalued candidates and verify strong fundamentals, the next step is to estimate what the asset is *truly worth*. This is the heart of the BL–SH System because it transforms vague judgment into measurable opportunity.

Fair value does not need to be perfect. It needs to be **reasonable, conservative, and repeatable** — something you can calculate across hundreds of assets with confidence.

The goal of fair-value estimation is simple:

Determine what the asset is worth so you know when price is cheap or expensive.

Fair value estimation is not about predicting the exact future. It is about creating a grounded baseline that anchors your decisions and removes emotional guesswork.

This step uses four simple, replicable models that work across stocks, crypto (where applicable), indices, commodities, and real estate.

1. Valuation Multiple Models (Simple, Fast, Reliable)

Multiple-based valuation is the simplest and most scalable method for estimating fair value.

Common multiples include:

- Price-to-Earnings (P/E)
- Price-to-Book (P/B)
- EV/EBITDA
- Free Cash Flow Yield

How it works:

1. Identify the company's **historical valuation range**.
2. Identify **peer group averages**.
3. Identify **market-cycle adjustments** (is the sector in fear or hype?).
4. Assign a **conservative fair-value multiple**.

Example:

If the company historically trades at:

- 15–22× earnings in stable conditions,
- and currently trades at 9× earnings,

then fair value likely sits in the 14–18× range.

This immediately reveals whether the stock is priced:

- 20–50% below fair value (LOW zone),
- or 40–100% above fair value (HIGH zone).

2. Discounted Cash Flow "Lite" (DCF-Lite): Simple, Not Complex

A full DCF can be overly complicated, subjective, and fragile. A simplified DCF is far more powerful for everyday use — it focuses on the two variables that matter most:

1. projected cash flow,
2. a conservative discount rate.

The DCF-Lite Formula (conceptual):

$$\text{Fair Value} = \frac{\text{FCF}}{\text{Discount Rate} - \text{Growth}}$$

This model is stable when:

- growth assumptions are conservative,
- discount rates reflect realistic risk,
- terminal growth is modest,
- no heroic assumptions are used.

Practical approach:

- Use last year's free cash flow.
- Apply 0–3% long-term growth.
- Use 10–12% discount rate for equities (higher for riskier assets).

This gives you a solid, conservative fair-value anchor.

3. Earnings Power Model (EPM): The Buffett Method

Buffett's favorite valuation approach is simple:

1. Assess normalized earnings (5-year average).
2. Apply a reasonable earnings multiple (e.g., 12–18×).

Why this works:

- smooths out temporary spikes or drops,
- focuses on long-term earning capacity,
- avoids dependence on short-term forecasts.

If normalized earnings are stable and price trades far below the implied range, you have a HIGH-probability LOW-zone candidate.

4. Relative Value: What Is Cheap Compared to Peers?

Relative-value models tell you whether the asset is cheap or expensive compared to others in the same sector or category.

Compare:

- valuation multiples,
- margins,
- growth rates,
- debt profiles,
- profitability.

If a company is:

- cheaper,
- stronger,
- more profitable,

than its peers, it is likely undervalued.

Why Simple Models Work Best

Complex models introduce:

- more assumptions,
- more noise,
- more ways to be wrong.

Simple models:

- keep thinking clear,
- eliminate bias,
- allow fast iteration,
- are highly scalable across many assets.

The BL–SH System prioritizes models that are:

1. simple,
2. conservative,
3. easy to replicate,
4. hard to manipulate emotionally.

Building a Fair-Value Range, Not a Single Number

Fair value is not a precise point — it is a zone.

Create a range:

- **Lower bound:** highly conservative estimate
- **Upper bound:** reasonable optimistic estimate

Price becomes attractive when:

$$\text{Price} \leq \text{Lower Fair-Value Bound}$$

Price becomes dangerous when:

$$\text{Price} \geq \text{Upper Fair-Value Bound}$$

How Fair Value Fits Into the BL–SH System

You scan for undervaluation (Step 1). You validate fundamentals (Step 2). You estimate fair value (Step 3).

Only then can you execute Step 4: **Enter in the LOW-Zone** — when price trades below fair value, fear is elevated, and fundamentals are strong.

Fair value estimation protects you from:

- chasing hype,
- buying falling knives,
- overpaying for growth,
- misreading sentiment,
- emotional decision-making.

Fair value is your anchor. Without it, the market pushes you around.

Next we move to Step 4: entering at the optimal point — the LOW-Zone.

6.4 Step 4 — Enter in the LOW-Zone

The purpose of the first three steps—scanning, validating fundamentals, and estimating fair value—is to bring you to this moment: the moment of entry. This is where discipline matters most and where most investors fail.

Entering in the LOW-Zone is the core of the Buy Low–Sell High System. It is where asymmetric opportunity appears:

- limited downside,

- large upside,
- strong fundamentals,
- fear-driven mispricing.

The LOW-Zone is not a random dip. It is not "the chart looks low." It is not buying because price fell.

The LOW-Zone occurs when a very specific set of conditions align:

$$\text{Price is below Fair Value} + \text{Fundamentals Strong} + \text{Fear Present}$$

Nothing less qualifies.

This section teaches you exactly how to identify the LOW-Zone and how to enter with precision, confidence, and discipline.

1. Price Must Be Below Fair Value — The Golden Rule

The essence of buying low is simple:

Never buy an asset above its fair value.
Only buy when market price trades at a discount.

This discount is your margin of safety — the cushion that protects you against uncertainty, volatility, and temporary errors.

Your ideal discount range:

- **20–40% below fair value:** Strong LOW-Zone
- **40–70% below fair value:** Deep LOW-Zone (rare, powerful)

Why a discount matters:

- It reduces downside risk.
- It amplifies long-term compounding.
- It gives room for valuation normalization.
- It allows recovery even if fundamentals improve slowly.

Buying without a discount is gambling. Buying with a discount is strategy.

2. Fundamentals Must Be Intact — Discount Without Damage

A LOW-Zone exists only if the underlying asset remains fundamentally healthy.

This means:

- stable revenue,
- manageable debt,
- strong cash flow,
- real moat,
- no structural decline.

If price is low because the business is collapsing → this is a value trap, not a LOW-Zone.

3. Fear or Panic Must Be Present — Emotional Mispricing

A true LOW-Zone is not created by numbers alone. It is created by psychology.

Look for fear-driven triggers:

- market-wide panic,
- temporary controversy,
- earnings overreaction,
- short-term bad news,
- regulatory shocks,
- misunderstood events.

Fear creates the discount. Fundamentals make the discount attractive.

4. Price Behavior Must Show Exhaustion — Selling Pressure Weakening

Even when price trades below value, you do not enter blindly. You enter when selling pressure starts to decline.

Technical confirmations:

- RSI deeply oversold (¡30 or ¡20),
- VIX or volatility spike fading,
- long wicks showing failed downward moves,

- stabilization near support,
- volume drying up on selling days,
- higher lows forming.

Buying during the middle of a panic is dangerous. Buying after panic exhausts is powerful.

5. Build Your Entry Plan — With Precision

Your entry plan should include:

- the exact price range you want,
- scaling strategy (one shot vs multiple buys),
- position size limit,
- risk parameters,
- criteria that would invalidate the entry (e.g., fundamental deterioration).

Scaling helps avoid uncertainty:

- Buy 30–50% on initial LOW-Zone signal.
- Add more if price falls further but fundamentals remain intact.
- Add final portion on trend confirmation.

This keeps you flexible and protects you from overcommitting too early.

6. Emotionless Execution — The Purpose of Steps 1–3

By the time you reach Step 4:

- you know the asset is undervalued,
- you know fundamentals are strong,
- you know fair value,
- you know the discount,
- you know fear is driving mispricing.

This eliminates hesitation. It eliminates FOMO buying. It eliminates panic buying or selling.

You are no longer reacting — you are executing a plan.

What the LOW-Zone Really Represents

The LOW-Zone is where the highest asymmetry exists:

$$\text{Small Risk} \longrightarrow \text{Large Reward}$$

$$\text{Temporary Fear} \longrightarrow \text{Long-Term Advantage}$$

$$\text{Discounted Price} \longrightarrow \text{Compounding Engine}$$

When you consistently enter in LOW-Zones, you no longer need to guess the future. The math works for you.

Why This Step Matters

Entering in the LOW-Zone is the most powerful part of the Buy Low–Sell High System because it ensures:

- you never overpay,
- you never chase hype,
- you buy with a margin of safety,
- you buy when others fear,
- you position yourself for outsized returns,
- you reduce emotional volatility,
- you stack probabilistic edges across cycles.

Buy Low is not a slogan. It is a disciplined entry protocol.

6.5 Step 5 — Set HIGH-Zone Exit Targets

Knowing when to sell is harder than knowing when to buy. Most investors give back their gains because they wait for "just a little more," or because they never define what "high" actually means. Greed replaces logic, optimism replaces discipline, and profits evaporate during the reversal.

The purpose of Step 5 is to eliminate all uncertainty and emotion from the selling process. You predetermine your exit targets *before* you buy — when your mind is calm, your thinking is rational, and your judgment is not influenced by price movement.

This transforms selling from a reaction into a system.

1. The Core Rule: Decide Your Exit Before You Enter

A disciplined investor never enters a position without knowing:

- where fair value is,
- where the HIGH zone begins,
- where profits should be locked,
- where the risk-reward flips,
- where the position becomes vulnerable.

This protects you from emotional biases:

- FOMO during parabolic rallies,
- greed during euphoric peaks,
- hesitation during distribution,
- denial during early declines.

When exit targets are decided in advance, you never have to think under pressure — you just execute the plan.

2. Build Your Exit Targets Around the HIGH-Zone Matrix

Your exit framework is built on the four pillars you learned earlier:

1. Overvaluation
2. Sentiment Extreme (Euphoria)
3. Price Acceleration
4. Smart Money Exiting

Your exit targets must reflect where these pillars tend to converge.

Define three ranges:

- **Range A: Fair Value Zone** Where price first meets your fair-value estimate. This is your baseline scaling-out level.
- **Range B: Mild Overvaluation Zone** Price trades above fair value by 10–25%. Sentiment rises, momentum accelerates.
- **Range C: High-Zone Cluster** Parabolic moves, extreme sentiment, and insider selling — the zone of maximum risk.

Your exit plan should operate across these zones.

3. The Two-Part Exit Architecture: Target Exit + Conditional Exit

A complete exit plan has two components:

a. Target-Based Exit

This is based on numbers and valuation:

- Price reaches fair value → partial exit.
- Price exceeds fair value → further reduction.
- Price enters HIGH zone → major exit.

You predetermine:

- your target price levels,
- what percentage to sell at each level.

b. Condition-Based Exit

This is based on behavior and psychology:

- sentiment becomes euphoric,
- price accelerates parabolically,
- volume spikes then fades,
- insiders start selling,
- retail flows surge,
- news becomes excessively bullish,
- expectations become unrealistic.

Condition-based exits protect you even if price hasn't yet reached your numeric target.

4. Define Your Scaling-Out Framework

A smart exit is not a one-shot action — it is a sequence. Scaling out lets you:

- secure profits early,
- capture additional upside,
- protect capital during reversals,

- remove emotion from the process.

A simple, powerful structure:

- **First Exit (25–30%):** At or near fair value.
- **Second Exit (25–30%):** When price moves into mild overvaluation or early euphoria.
- **Final Exit (40–50%):** In the HIGH zone — parabolic price, extreme sentiment, insider selling.

If the asset becomes euphoric before reaching fair value, your condition-based exits take priority.

5. Build Your Exit Target Table

Before entering any position, create a simple table:

Zone	Sell Action
Fair Value	Sell 25–30%
Mild Overvaluation (+10–25%)	Sell 25–30%
HIGH-Zone Cluster	Sell 40–50% or exit fully
Parabolic Move + Euphoria	Immediate reduction
Insider Selling Spike	Protective exit

This table makes selling automatic.

6. Why Predetermining Exit Targets Creates Discipline

Setting exit targets in advance protects you from:

- greed,
- hesitation,
- emotional attachment,
- anchoring,
- unrealistic expectations,
- crowd influence,
- narrative traps.

When price rises, you don't ask:

"Should I sell now?"

You simply follow your plan.

7. Predetermined Exits Create Asymmetry

With exit targets:

- your downside is protected,
- your profits are realized systematically,
- your emotional stability increases,
- your compounding accelerates,
- your long-term returns become more consistent.

You stop trying to catch the exact top. You capture the bulk of the move — and protect capital before reversals.

Step 5 Completing the BL–SH Cycle

This step is the bridge between entry and compounding. Without predetermined exit targets, even perfect LOW-zone entries can fail.

You cannot control the market. You can control your exits.

Next we move to Step 6: **Scaling-Out Profit Taking** — the engine of long-term consistency.

6.6 Step 6 — Scale-Out Profit Taking

Taking profits is where discipline turns paper gains into realized returns. A single perfect entry can be ruined by a single late exit. Scaling out — selling in planned tranches — protects gains, reduces regret, and preserves optionality to capture further upside. This section explains a clear, repeatable scale-out protocol and the practical mechanics for executing it across asset classes.

Core Principle

Realize gains early, protect the remainder.
Sell a defined portion at valuation targets (25–50%), and manage the remainder with a trailing stop or rule-based protection.

This approach balances two competing objectives:

- **Lock profits** — crystallize returns so you cannot give them back.
- **Capture upside** — remain exposed to further appreciation without risking the entire position.

A Simple, Robust Scaling Framework

Use a three-tranche model as your baseline. Adjust percentages to fit your risk tolerance and portfolio sizing rules.

- **Tranche A — Realize (25–30%):** Sell the first slice when price reaches your fair value estimate. This converts a portion of the position to cash and covers opportunity cost and taxes.
- **Tranche B — Rotate (25–30%):** Sell the second slice in the mild overvaluation / early euphoria range (e.g., 10–25% above fair value) or when sentiment signals strengthen.
- **Tranche C — Protect (40–50%):** Manage the remainder with a trailing stop or dynamic hedge to lock gains while allowing for continued upside.

Adjust percentages based on conviction, liquidity and portfolio rules. For high-conviction core holdings you may reduce immediate realization and push more to the trailing stop; for speculative positions increase realization.

When to Execute Each Tranche

Tranche A (Fair Value). Execute when price reaches the lower bound of your fair-value range. This is the most mechanical sell and should be entered as a limit order or scheduled VWAP slice to avoid slippage.

Tranche B (Mild Overvaluation). Execute when either (a) price exceeds the upper bound of fair value by a pre-specified band (e.g., +10–25%), or (b) early signs of euphoria / momentum appear (rising media attention, strong inflows). Use limit or staged orders to sell into strength.

Tranche C (Trailing / Protect). Convert the last tranche to a protected position using a trailing stop, hedge (options), or dynamic rebalancing. Choose an approach that fits liquidity and volatility characteristics of the asset.

Trailing Stop Methods — Practical Options

Choose a trailing stop method that matches the asset's volatility and your holding horizon.

- **Percentage trailing stop:** Simple (e.g., 15–30% below peak). Works well for less volatile blue-chips.
- **ATR-based trailing stop:** Use multiple of Average True Range (e.g., 2–4× ATR) to allow for normal noise while protecting gains.
- **Moving average stop:** Exit when price closes below a moving average (50-day or 100-day) — useful for trend trades.

- **Time-based step-down:** Gradually tighten stops as time passes or as sentiment signals increase.
- **Options hedge:** Buy protective puts for the remainder instead of hard exit (costly but keeps upside intact).

Use ATR or volatility scaling for small-cap / crypto where fixed percentages either stop you out too early or allow too much drawdown.

Execution Tactics and Market Impact

- **Limit vs Market:** Prefer limit orders when liquidity is thin; use market orders only to ensure execution in a fast reversal.
- **VWAP / TWAP slicing:** For large blocks, slice execution across the day (VWAP/TWAP) to avoid moving the market.
- **Block trades:** Consider block trades or dark pools for very large positions to reduce signaling risk.
- **Watch liquidity windows:** Avoid selling large portions into illiquid pre-open/close spreads unless necessary.

Psychology and Behavioral Rules

- **Pre-commitment:** Define scale out rules before entering the trade. This removes second-guessing during rallies.
- **Avoid perfectionism:** Capturing the majority of gains consistently beats trying to catch the exact top.
- **Document decisions:** Log why you sold each tranche (valuation, sentiment, price action). This builds discipline and improves future choices.
- **Be tax-aware:** Know your jurisdiction's tax rules (short vs long term). Taxes can influence the slice sizes and timing.

Examples (Illustrative Numbers)

Example A — Single stock purchase:

- Buy 1000 shares at \$50 (cost basis \$50,000). Fair value estimated at \$80.
- Tranche A (25%): sell 250 shares at \$80 → realize \$20,000.
- Tranche B (25%): sell 250 shares at \$96 (+20%) → realize \$24,000.
- Tranche C (50%): hold 500 shares with 20% trailing stop from peak; if peak \$120, stop triggers at \$96, or hedge with puts.

Example B — Crypto / High volatility:

- Smaller tranche sizes (20/30/50) but use ATR-based trailing stop (e.g., $3\times$ ATR) instead of simple
- Use staged limit sells across volume spikes to minimize slippage.

Special Cases and Adjustments

- **Illiquid assets / private deals:** Scale out via staged secondary sales or structured buyouts; use negotiated exits, not market orders.
- **Dividend / income holdings:** You may hold a larger core for yield; realize profits from a tradable tranche only.
- **Tax-efficient harvesting:** If holding long term, sell tax-loss winners/losers strategically across years to optimize after-tax returns.
- **Core vs Satellite:** For core portfolio holdings (buy-and-hold), use wider stops and smaller tranche realization; for satellite speculative positions, realize earlier and larger.

When to Deviate — and When Not To

Deviations are allowed only with pre-defined, objective triggers (e.g., material change in fundamentals, acquisition offer, or regulatory shock). Avoid emotional overrides. Any deviation must be documented and reviewed in the post-mortem.

Reinvestment and Rotation

Proceeds from realized tranches should be:

- redeployed into other LOW-zone opportunities, or
- used to rebalance the portfolio to target allocations, or
- kept as dry powder for future accumulation.

Plan the reuse of proceeds in advance to avoid impulse redeployment into euphoric assets.

Record-Keeping and Review

Maintain a simple trade log:

- entry price, size, date, thesis,
- tranche sell prices, sizes, reasons,
- trailing stop settings / hedge details,

- post-trade review notes (what went right/wrong).

Quarterly or semi-annual post-mortems refine your scale-out rules and improve long-term performance.

Summary — The Purpose of Scale-Out Profit Taking

- Scale-outs lock gains while preserving upside.
- Predefined tranches (25–50%) plus a protected remainder create symmetry between capturing returns and protecting capital.
- Use volatility-adjusted trailing stops, execution tactics, and documentation to make exits disciplined and repeatable.
- The output of disciplined scale-outs: more realized returns, less psychological stress, and a higher probability of compounding wealth over time.

6.7 Step 7 — Repeat the Cycle

Buying well, selling well, and managing positions well matter — but compounding only begins when you repeat the process consistently across cycles.

Step 7 is the engine of long-term wealth creation. It transforms isolated wins into exponential growth. It is where discipline becomes destiny.

Most investors treat Buy–Sell decisions as one-time events. Great investors treat them as a continuous loop — a repeating system that harvests opportunity and reinvests it again and again.

1. Compounding Comes From Repetition, Not Perfection

Compounding does not require:

- perfect entries,
- perfect exits,
- perfect timing,
- perfect predictions.

It requires:

- consistently buying below value,
- consistently selling above value,
- protecting gains,
- reinvesting profits.

Compounding is the mathematical reward for emotional discipline.

2. Repetition Converts Market Cycles Into Wealth Cycles

Every market cycle has:

- fear → LOW zones,
- euphoria → HIGH zones,
- crashes → reset points,
- recoveries → early opportunities.

When you repeat the BL–SH loop through multiple cycles, each cycle reinforces the next:

Accumulate in fear → Exit in greed → Reinvest in fear → Exit in greed.

You climb the staircase of wealth one cycle at a time.

3. Reinvesting Is the Secret to Exponential Growth

Selling high creates realized profits. But profits only compound when they are reinvested into new undervalued assets.

Flow of capital in the BL–SH System:

1. Buy undervalued assets
2. Sell in the HIGH zone
3. Move profits to cash or short-term instruments
4. Scan again for new LOW-zone opportunities
5. Deploy capital into the next cycle

This loop multiplies your capital base over time.

4. Each Cycle Strengthens Your Edge

With each completed BL–SH cycle, you:

- refine your valuation judgment,
- recognize LOW-zone signals faster,
- spot HIGH-zone signals earlier,
- strengthen emotional discipline,
- build confidence in your process,
- eliminate weak habits and decisions.

Your system improves because you improve.

5. Build a Compounding Journal

Track each cycle:

- entry details and rationale,
- exit details and signals,
- what worked, what didn't,
- cycle timing,
- behavior mistakes,
- return on capital,
- lessons extracted.

This transforms experience into wisdom — and wisdom into better future cycles.

6. The Math of Repeating Edges

If you systematically:

- enter with a 20–50% discount,
- exit with 20–50% premium,
- redeploy profits,
- avoid large losses,

your wealth trajectory becomes exponential, even with modest accuracy. A few high-quality cycles outperform decades of random trading.

7. The Psychological Advantage of a Repeatable Cycle

Repetition creates:

- calm during crashes,
- clarity during rallies,
- confidence during uncertainty.

When you've lived through multiple cycles, you stop fearing volatility — you start recognizing opportunity.

8. Why Repetition Is the Heart of the BL–SH System

This system is not a prediction model. It is a compounding machine.

Your job is not to forecast the future.
Your job is to repeat the process.

Each completed cycle increases:

- your capital,
- your discipline,
- your skill,
- your ability to act rationally,
- your long-term returns.

The Cycle Never Ends — And That's the Power

Markets will always generate:

- fear,
- greed,
- mispricing,
- opportunities.

When you follow a system built on buying undervaluation, selling overvaluation, and repeating consistently across decades, wealth becomes a natural by-product.

Repetition turns Buy Low–Sell High from a rule into a lifestyle.
This is where compounding happens.

Key Takeaways

- **The BL–SH System transforms Buy Low–Sell High into a repeatable process.** It replaces emotion and improvisation with structure, clarity, and discipline.
- **Step 1: Scan for undervalued assets.** Use simple, powerful tools — P/E, P/B, FCF yield, RSI, volatility — to identify candidates trading below intrinsic worth.

- **Step 2: Validate fundamentals.** Strong revenue, manageable debt, consistent cash flow, and a defensible moat separate undervalued opportunities from value traps.
- **Step 3: Estimate fair value.** Use simple, replicable models (multiples, DCF-lite, earnings power, relative value) to build a conservative fair-value range.
- **Step 4: Enter in the LOW-Zone.** Only buy when price trades *below* fair value, fundamentals are strong, and fear-driven mispricing is present.
- **Step 5: Set HIGH-Zone exit targets before entering.** Predetermined exit levels eliminate emotional selling errors and allow disciplined profit realization.
- **Step 6: Scale-out profit taking.** Sell 25–50% around valuation targets and manage the rest with trailing stops to lock gains while capturing further upside.
- **Step 7: Repeat the cycle.** Long-term compounding comes from repeating systematic entries and exits across many cycles — not from predicting tops and bottoms.
- **Consistency beats perfection.** You do not need perfect timing; you need a repeatable edge applied with discipline.
- **The system protects you from psychological biases.** Predefined steps outperform fear, greed, FOMO, and hesitation.
- **Compounding is the mathematical reward for emotional discipline.** When you repeat the BL–SH cycle for years and decades, wealth grows exponentially.

This chapter gives you the complete operational blueprint. The next chapters show you how to apply it across real market cycles and asset classes.

Chapter 7

The 12-Minute Execution Routine

A great system is useless without consistent execution. The BL–SH Method gives you the strategy; this routine makes it effortless to follow.

The 12-Minute Execution Routine is your lifelong operating rhythm — a simple, fast, structured process that keeps you aligned with the Buy Low–Sell High system without overwhelming your time or attention.

In just twelve minutes, you stay disciplined, aware, and in control:

- **Daily (3 minutes):** Track sentiment and price movement to spot emotional extremes.
- **Weekly (6 minutes):** Review fundamentals and valuation to ensure your positions still deserve to be held.
- **Monthly (3 minutes):** Evaluate HIGH-zone exit conditions, rebalance, and redirect capital to new opportunities.

This chapter turns the entire book into a practical, repeatable habit — a routine you can follow forever, regardless of market conditions.

7.1 Daily (3 Minutes): Check Sentiment + Price Movement

Your daily routine is intentionally minimal. In just three minutes, you perform a quick scan that keeps you anchored to reality, aware of emotional extremes, and aligned with the BL–SH System — without falling into the trap of over-monitoring markets.

The daily check is not about making decisions. It is about maintaining awareness.

1. Read the Emotional Temperature of the Market

Sentiment drives short-term price distortions. A fast sentiment scan tells you whether the market is:

- fearful (potential LOW-zone opportunities forming),
- euphoric (HIGH-zone conditions building),
- neutral (no action required).

Tools you glance at:

- Fear/Greed Index
- Volatility Index (VIX or equivalent)
- Market heatmap (green/red intensity)
- Headlines tone (fear or excitement)
- Social chatter tone (panic or FOMO)

This takes under a minute.

2. Check Price Movement — Only to Spot Extremes

You are not looking for patterns. You are looking for outliers.

What you scan:

- Your watchlist or portfolio,
- Any asset dropping sharply (could be fear-based),
- Any asset rising sharply (could be euphoric),
- Sectors showing unusual volatility,
- Breakdowns or breakouts that change context.

Again, the goal is not action — only situational awareness.

3. Identify Anything That Needs Observation Later

If you notice:

- panic-level drops,
- sudden spikes,
- sentiment extremes,
- news-driven selloffs,
- early signs of euphoria,

you simply flag them for the weekly review. No decisions. No trades. No emotional reactions.

4. Why the Daily Routine Works

The power of this 3-minute check is psychological:

- It keeps you engaged without causing stress.
- It prevents reactive decisions.
- It sharpens your intuition over time.
- It keeps you aligned with market context.
- It replaces doom-scrolling with structured awareness.

You stay informed without being consumed.

5. The Golden Rule of the Daily Check

Observe daily. Act weekly or monthly.

Your job each day is simply to notice shifts in sentiment and price tone — not to respond emotionally or impulsively.

This 3-minute ritual builds the mental calm that allows the BL–SH System to work over decades.

7.2 Weekly (6 Minutes): Review Fundamentals & Valuation

The weekly check is where strategy meets verification. In six minutes you confirm that your positions still deserve to be held, that new candidates remain attractive, and that nothing in the business or valuation has changed materially since you last looked. This is not deep research — it is a focused maintenance routine designed to catch real risks and prevent slow drift into complacency.

Split the six minutes into three clear steps so the review stays fast, objective, and repeatable.

Minute 0–2: Quick Fundamentals Scan (2 minutes)

Purpose: confirm there are no sudden, material changes to the business.

Checklist (fast pass):

- **Revenue / Guidance changes:** any adjustments to quarterly guidance or surprising revenue beats/misses?
- **Cash / Liquidity:** are cash balances, credit lines, or liquidity signals materially different?

- **Debt events:** new debt issuance, covenant breaches, or large maturities coming due?
- **Operational flags:** major executive departures, regulatory actions, product failures, or recalls?
- **Earnings communications:** any new press releases, earnings previews, or conference-call highlights that change the thesis?

Action rules:

- If **no** material changes — mark "OK" and move on.
- If **minor** issues (explainable, temporary) — flag for deeper review and note a monitoring trigger (price or date).
- If **major** issues (fundamentals broken) — initiate exit protocol per your risk rules.

Minute 2–4: Valuation Check (2 minutes)

Purpose: confirm price still sits within your fair-value range or that movement suggests rebalancing.

Checklist (fast pass):

- **Price vs Fair-Value Range:** price below lower bound / within range / above upper bound?
- **Multiple movement:** has P/E, EV/EBITDA, or FCF yield moved materially relative to your baseline?
- **Peer divergence:** has the asset become materially richer or cheaper versus peers?
- **Macro drivers:** any macro change (rates, FX, commodity prices) that re-rates the sector?

Action rules:

- **Price falls into deeper LOW zone:** if fundamentals intact, consider adding per your scale-in plan (document amount and trigger).
- **Price rises toward/above upper fair-value bound:** prepare scale-out actions or tighten protection (advance your exit schedule).
- **Valuation unchanged:** no action; keep position and note next review date.

Minute 4–6: Tactical Actions and Scheduling (2 minutes)

Purpose: convert the scan into immediate, low-friction tasks and reminders so nothing is forgotten.

Routine tasks (fast execution):

- **Update trade log:** one-line note (status — OK / Flagged / Action) and reason.
- **Set or adjust alerts:** price alerts (entry/add, exit/trim), news alerts, and calendar reminders for deeper reviews.
- **Adjust risk controls:** update trailing stops, hedge size, or position size if your rules require it.
- **Schedule follow-up:** assign a single follow-up task (deeper analysis, call with advisor, read transcript) with a specific date.

When to escalate immediately:

- Evidence of a permanent fundamental change (revenue collapse, insolvency risk).
- Large valuation expansion without substantive fundamental improvement.
- Insider selling or institutional distribution that contradicts your thesis.

Practical Tips to Keep It to Six Minutes

- **Prepare a single dashboard:** one page (or one broker/watchlist view) that shows price, fair-value range, one-line fundamentals, and next action. Open it first thing.
- **Use templates:** a single-line weekly note template reduces decision friction: `Ticker | Price vs FV | Fund. OK/Flag | Action`.
- **Avoid research rabbit holes:** if an item needs more than two minutes, schedule a deeper review slot rather than doing it in the weekly scan.
- **Automate alerts:** let technology catch routine threshold crossings so your weekly check focuses on judgement calls.

Examples of Weekly Decisions

- **Example A (Positive):** Price drops 25% into deeper LOW zone; fundamentals unchanged → add 10% of planned allocation per scale-in rule; set next check in 2 weeks.

- **Example B (Caution):** Price rises 30% near upper FV bound and media tone shifts euphoric → sell 25% per exit table and tighten trailing stop on remainder.
- **Example C (Escalate):** Company misses guidance and cuts outlook; debt ratios worsen → follow exit protocol and schedule immediate full analysis.

Why the Weekly Review Is Critical

Daily scans keep you aware; monthly checks set strategy. The weekly routine is the operational link that turns awareness into disciplined, timely action. It prevents slow drift, catches early deterioration, and ensures you act on valuation movement before emotion forces reactive decisions.

Six minutes a week protects years of compounding.

7.3 Monthly (3 Minutes): Evaluate HIGH-Zone Exits & Rebalance

The monthly routine is the most strategic part of the 12-Minute Execution System. This is where you step back from short-term noise and evaluate your positions through the lens of the HIGH-Zone Matrix, ensuring that profits are protected and your capital remains allocated to the best opportunities available.

In just three minutes, you perform two critical tasks:

1. Evaluate whether any position is entering or approaching the HIGH zone.
2. Rebalance your portfolio toward undervalued, high-conviction opportunities.

This is the checkpoint that turns discipline into compounding.

1. HIGH-Zone Evaluation (2 Minutes)

The core purpose of this monthly check is to identify positions that are:

- overvalued,
- euphoric,
- accelerating unsustainably,
- showing signs of insider or institutional distribution.

You are looking for the alignment of the four HIGH-Zone pillars:

1. **Overvaluation** — price trades above the upper fair-value range.
2. **Sentiment Extreme** — excitement, headlines, social buzz, FOMO.
3. **Price Acceleration** — parabolic or unusually sharp rises.
4. **Smart Money Exiting** — insider selling or institutional trimming.

You evaluate each position through these lenses:
Checklist (60–90 seconds):

- Current price relative to your fair-value range (below, near, above, far above).
- Recent price acceleration (straight-line upward move? unusually fast?).
- News and sentiment tone (is the asset now "everywhere"?).
- Insider/institutional activity (selling, distribution spikes).
- Volume and participation (is retail buying aggressively?).

Action Rules:

- **If 0–1 HIGH-Zone signals:** Hold. No action.
- **If 2–3 signals:** Prepare scale-out orders; tighten trailing stops.
- **If 4+ signals:** Execute HIGH-Zone exits immediately per Step 6 rules.

This 2-minute evaluation ensures you never get blindsided by euphoric tops.

2. Rebalancing (1 Minute)

Rebalancing is where you redirect capital from strong performers to undervalued, high-conviction opportunities — the engine of long-term compounding.

This is not about selling losers; it's about reallocating from HIGH-zone assets to LOW-zone assets.

Checklist (45 seconds):

- Any position now overweight due to recent gains?
- Any position's fundamentals deteriorated?
- Any new LOW-zone opportunities from the past month?
- Portfolio balance vs your target allocation (equities, sectors, risk levels)?

Action Rules:

- Trim overweight positions (especially those with HIGH-zone signals).

- Redeploy proceeds into undervalued assets with strong fundamentals.
- If no new opportunities, keep excess in cash — dry powder for next LOW zone.

Rebalancing once a month prevents:

- concentration risk,
- emotional attachment,
- portfolio drift,
- overexposure to euphoric assets.

3. Why Monthly Review Works

A monthly interval is perfect because:

- Fundamental changes do not happen daily.
- Valuation shifts become visible over weeks, not hours.
- Sentiment extremes reveal themselves clearly across 30-day cycles.
- It avoids overtrading and impulse reactions.

This cadence ensures you remain strategic, not reactive.

4. Psychological Benefits

The monthly routine:

- removes the urge to chase tops,
- ensures your exits are rule-based,
- prevents you from holding "too long",
- keeps you excited about finding new opportunities,
- reduces the emotional load of decision-making.

It reinforces the identity of becoming a disciplined, system-oriented investor.

5. The Purpose of the Monthly Review

This part of the routine turns the entire BL–SH Method into a compounding machine by systematically reallocating capital from high-risk, overvalued assets to low-risk, undervalued opportunities.

Three minutes a month keeps you out of euphoria and aligned with compounding.

Key Takeaways

- **Execution beats intention.** The BL–SH System becomes powerful only when paired with a simple, consistent routine.
- **The 12-Minute Routine keeps you disciplined without overwhelming your time.** Three minutes daily, six minutes weekly, three minutes monthly — enough to stay aligned, aware, and in control.
- **Daily (3 minutes):** You check sentiment and price movement only to understand market emotion, not to make decisions. Awareness, not action.
- **Weekly (6 minutes):** You review fundamentals and valuation to ensure your holdings still deserve capital. This prevents drift, complacency, and silent fundamental decay.
- **Monthly (3 minutes):** You evaluate HIGH-zone exit conditions and rebalance toward undervalued assets. This protects profits and fuels compounding.
- **Minimal time, maximum leverage.** The routine gives you the benefits of active monitoring without the stress or noise of constant market watching.
- **System ¿ impulse.** You act weekly or monthly — never react daily. This removes emotional decisions from your investing life.
- **The routine is a lifelong habit.** It gives structure, confidence, and clarity across all market cycles and keeps your behavior aligned with the Buy Low–Sell High philosophy.
- **Consistency compounds.** Following the routine every month for years leads to better decisions, stronger discipline, and exponential long-term returns.

This chapter turns the entire book from theory into practice — a routine you can follow forever.

Chapter 8

Case Studies

The best way to understand a system is to watch it unfold in the real world. This chapter brings the BL–SH Method to life through clear, structured case studies that show how LOW signals, HIGH signals, and market psychology play out across different assets and cycles.

Each case study follows a simple, repeatable format:

- **LOW Signal** — what fear, valuation, and fundamentals looked like.
- **HIGH Signal** — what euphoria, acceleration, and narrative excess looked like.
- **What Happened** — how the cycle played out.
- **Lessons Learned** — the patterns you can reuse forever.

You will explore iconic cycles such as: Amazon's early 2000s recovery, Bitcoin's major bottoms, Tesla's mania, ITC's multi-year turnaround, PSU banks' revival, RIL's growth cycle, and more.

These stories reveal a single truth: **Patterns repeat. Behavior repeats. LOW → HIGH is universal.** This chapter shows you how to recognize it in the wild.

8.1 Amazon (2001–2006)

Amazon's early 2000s cycle is one of the purest Buy Low–Sell High examples in modern market history. It shows how fear creates deep undervaluation, how fundamentals quietly strengthen beneath the panic, and how euphoria eventually returns in predictable waves.

This case study follows the four-part model: **LOW Signal → HIGH Signal → What Happened → Lessons Learned.**

1. LOW Signal: 2001–2002 — "This company will not survive."

After the dot-com crash, Amazon fell from over $100 to nearly $6. The market believed:

- Amazon would run out of cash,
- e-commerce would die,
- online retail was a bubble,
- unprofitable tech had no future.

Sentiment was catastrophic. Analysts declared the business "dead." Headlines predicted bankruptcy. Investors abandoned all internet companies.

But fundamentals told a different story:

- Revenue was still growing.
- Customer base was expanding.
- Losses were shrinking quarter by quarter.
- Operational efficiency was improving.
- Gross margins were rising.

Valuation was absurdly low:

- Price-to-sales collapsed to $1\times$.
- Market cap fell below the value of its long-term potential.
- Cash position was stronger than headlines suggested.

LOW-Zone Characteristics Present:

- Price far below intrinsic value.
- Fundamentals quietly strengthening.
- Fear and panic dominating decisions.
- No narrative support — only despair.

This was a textbook LOW zone hiding in plain sight.

2. HIGH Signal: 2005–2006 — "Amazon is unstoppable."

By 2005–2006, the story had completely flipped.

Price surged more than 10× from the bottom. Euphoria began returning to tech. Amazon was no longer seen as a risky experiment — it was seen as the future.

Sentiment reached optimism:

- Analysts upgraded targets aggressively.
- Media stories praised Amazon's strategy.
- Retail investors again poured into tech stocks.

Valuation stretched:

- Price-to-sales expanded massively.
- Investors priced in years of growth.
- "This time it's different" narratives resurfaced.

HIGH-Zone Characteristics Present:

- Euphoria and confidence everywhere.
- Price acceleration created unrealistic expectations.
- Risk-reward shifted — upside already priced in.
- Smart money quietly took profits.

This was a classic early HIGH zone: confidence ¿ fundamentals.

3. What Happened: The Cycle in Motion

From 2001 to 2006, Amazon moved through a full BL–SH cycle:

- **Fear Phase (2001–2002):** Price collapsed. Fundamentals held steady. The best opportunity.
- **Recovery Phase (2003–2004):** Revenue grew. Costs fell. The market ignored the improvement.
- **Momentum Phase (2004–2005):** Price ran ahead of fundamentals as the narrative turned positive.
- **Euphoria Phase (2005–2006):** Valuations expanded aggressively. LONG holders took profits.

Those who bought when fear was extreme and sold into optimism made 8–12× returns. Those who entered during euphoria earned far less and faced heavy drawdowns.

4. Lessons Learned: The Universal Pattern

Amazon's cycle illustrates principles that repeat across all markets:

- **LOW zones always look like death.** Fear blinds the crowd to improving fundamentals.
- **Fundamental improvement begins before price improvement.** Markets react late.
- **Euphoria always returns.** Narratives flip faster than fundamentals.
- **The crowd buys at the wrong part of the cycle.** Most retail money flowed in during 2005–2006 — not 2001–2002.
- **Valuation cycles exaggerate both fear and confidence.** Price moved far below and far above intrinsic value.
- **The BL–SH pattern is timeless.** Strong business + temporary panic = deep opportunity.

Amazon 2001–2006 is proof that the BL–SH System works even in the most emotional, chaotic markets.

8.2 Bitcoin Bottoms (2018, 2020, 2022)

Bitcoin has one of the clearest and most emotionally extreme boom–bust cycles in modern market history. Its bottoms across 2018, 2020, and 2022 demonstrate the BL–SH System perfectly: deep undervaluation driven by fear, followed by explosive recovery driven by narrative and liquidity.

This case study follows the four-part structure: **LOW Signal → HIGH Signal → What Happened → Lessons Learned.**

1. LOW Signal (2018): "Crypto is dead."

After the 2017 mania (Bitcoin hitting $20,000), the market reversed violently.

Sentiment Collapsed:

- Headlines declared the entire crypto industry a fraud.
- Retail investors capitulated.
- Governments threatened bans.
- Influencers disappeared.

Price Structure:

- Bitcoin fell from $20,000 to $3,100.

- Down 85% from the top.
- RSI hit extreme oversold zones.
- Volatility spiked during panic.

Fundamentals (Yes, Bitcoin Has Fundamentals):

- Network hash rate continued rising.
- Developer activity remained stable.
- User addresses and transactions grew.
- Institutional interest quietly began forming.

LOW-Zone Characteristics:

- Extreme fear.
- Forced liquidations.
- Price trading far below cost basis.
- Fundamentals unchanged or improving.

The 2018 bottom was a textbook LOW signal.

2. LOW Signal (2020): "Bitcoin will go to zero during Covid."

March 2020 brought a global liquidity crisis.

Sentiment Reset to Panic:

- Markets crashed globally.
- Bitcoin plunged from $10,000 to $3,800 in two days.
- Leverage washed out the system.

But fundamentals again remained strong:

- Halving was approaching (supply shock).
- Institutional allocation began accelerating.
- Long-term holders increased accumulation.

LOW-Zone Indicators:

- RSI extremely oversold.
- Volatility index at all-time high.
- Price below mining cost.
- Massive fear-driven liquidations.

Another textbook LOW zone created by global panic.

3. LOW Signal (2022): "Crypto is finished forever."

This bottom was created not by macro fear but by industry collapse:

- LUNA collapse,
- 3AC collapse,
- Celsius failure,
- FTX fraud exposure.

Sentiment Turned Nuclear:

- "Crypto is a scam."
- "Bitcoin will die."
- Regulatory pressure intensifying.
- Narratives predicting $1,000 Bitcoin.

Price Structure:

- Bitcoin fell from $69,000 to $15,476.
- Down 78% from the top.
- Capitulation candles everywhere.
- On-chain metrics signaled generational undervaluation.

Fundamentals Remained Powerful:

- Hash rate hit new highs.
- Long-term holders held ¿70% of supply.
- Institutional custody infrastructure continued expanding.
- Network adoption remained steady.

This was a deep, prolonged LOW zone defined by structural fear, not structural weakness.

4. HIGH Signal: The Pattern of Bitcoin Tops

Every Bitcoin cycle top shows identical HIGH-zone features:
2017, 2021, and future cycles all show:

- massive parabolic price acceleration,
- new retail participants entering late,
- mainstream media euphoria,

- celebrities and influencers promoting crypto,
- unrealistic narratives ("Bitcoin to $1 million next year!"),
- extremely stretched valuation relative to on-chain models,
- huge spike in leverage,
- smart money quietly distributing to retail buyers.

HIGH zones in Bitcoin are unmistakable: **speed + sentiment + liquidity mania.**

5. What Happened: The Results of the Three LOW Zones

From the 2018 bottom ($3,100):

- Bitcoin rallied to $69,000.
- 22× return.

From the 2020 bottom ($3,800):

- Bitcoin rallied to $64,000.
- 17× return.

From the 2022 bottom ($15,476):

- Bitcoin rallied to new cycle highs.
- Early profits already ¿3× in the following months.

Every LOW-zone buyer made life-changing returns. Every euphoria-zone buyer suffered brutal drawdowns.

6. Lessons Learned: The Bitcoin Pattern Is Universal

- **Bitcoin bottoms always occur during catastrophic sentiment.** When headlines say "Crypto is dead," the LOW zone is forming.
- **Fundamentals diverge from price during fear.** Hash rate, adoption, and long-term holder supply strengthen during bottoms.
- **Capitulation candles are opportunity signals.** Forced liquidations create undervaluation more than fundamental weakness.
- **Bitcoin tops always come with mania.** Euphoria, FOMO, and leverage mark every cycle peak.
- **The BL–SH pattern is consistent across cycles.** 2018, 2020, and 2022 bottoms share identical emotional and structural features.

- **Buying in fear works. Selling in euphoria works.** The system wins because human behavior is cyclical and predictable.

Bitcoin's history proves that even the most volatile asset follows the same LOW → HIGH cycles as every market in this book.

8.3 Tesla Mania (2020–2021)

Tesla's 2020–2021 cycle is one of the most dramatic examples of how euphoria, narrative, and acceleration convert a fundamentally strong company into a HIGH-zone frenzy. It shows how valuation detaches from reality, how crowds amplify stories into manias, and how smart money distributes quietly at the top.

This case study follows the four-part template: **LOW Signal → HIGH Signal → What Happened → Lessons Learned**.

1. LOW Signal: 2018–2019 — "Tesla will go bankrupt."

Before the mania, Tesla lived through a deep fear period.

Sentiment Was Extremely Negative:

- Analysts called Tesla "unprofitable forever."
- Media said the company would "run out of cash."
- Short-sellers predicted bankruptcy.
- Production delays created widespread panic.

Price Action:

- Tesla fell to the equivalent of \$35–\$40 pre-split.
- Market cap dropped to levels below long-term potential.
- Volatility spiked as uncertainty peaked.

Fundamentals Told a Different Story:

- Model 3 demand proved extremely strong.
- Gross margins improved.
- Cash burn reduced materially.
- Shanghai Gigafactory moved ahead of schedule.
- Regulatory credits boosted earnings.

Clear LOW-Zone Indicators:

- Fear-based selling.
- Misunderstood business model.
- Price well below future earning power.
- Sentiment at multi-year lows.

This was a classic "fear exaggerates the downside" moment.

2. HIGH Signal: 2020–2021 — One of the Greatest Manias of the Century

In 2020, everything flipped instantly. Fear turned into the strongest euphoria the EV sector had ever seen.

Price Acceleration:

- Tesla rose from \$100 (post-split) to \$1,200.
- More than 10× in 18 months.
- Parabolic rises across multiple waves.

Sentiment Reached Extreme Levels:

- Tesla became a cultural phenomenon.
- Retail traders flooded in after every rally.
- Social media declared Tesla "the future of everything."
- Analysts issued \$5,000 and \$7,000/share price targets.

Narrative Excess:

- "Tesla will own 100% of the EV market."
- "Tesla will replace all oil companies."
- "Full Self Driving is days away."
- "Tesla's true value is \$10 trillion."

Valuation Became Detached:

- P/E exceeded 1,000× at peak.
- Market cap ¿ combined value of all legacy automakers.
- Price implied dominance far beyond plausible reality.

Smart Money Exiting:

- Insiders and early employees sold massive amounts.

- Funds trimmed positions.
- Tesla issued new shares (capital raise) at peak valuations.

This was a perfect HIGH-zone cluster: **overvaluation + mania + narrative + insider selling.**

3. What Happened: The Full Mania–Correction Cycle

Mania Phase (2020–2021):

- Price went vertical.
- Retail investors entered aggressively.
- Leverage in options markets exploded.

Distribution Phase:

- Smart money sold into strength.
- Tesla raised billions in new capital.
- Momentum indicators peaked.

Correction Phase (2022):

- Price fell from \$1,200 → \$600 → \$300.
- Down 75% from peak.
- Long consolidation followed.

Outcome:

- Early buyers (2018–2019) still made 10×–20× returns.
- Mania buyers (late 2021) faced heavy drawdowns.
- Systematic sellers protected gains; emotional holders didn't.

4. Lessons Learned: Tesla Shows How HIGH Zones Unfold

a. LOW Zones Look Like Failure

Panic creates opportunity. Tesla's fundamentals were improving even when headlines said "bankrupt."

b. HIGH Zones Look Like Destiny

At the top:

- narratives become perfect,
- price accelerates beyond fundamentals,
- analysts become storytellers,
- retail participation peaks.

c. Valuation Always Matters — Eventually

Even the world's strongest companies cannot justify infinite valuations.

d. Mania Is Always Obvious — In Hindsight

Every mania has:

- parabolic charts,
- celebrity endorsements,
- new retail investors entering,
- extreme price-to-reality gaps.

Tesla's 2020–2021 cycle hit all four.

e. Smart Money Sells Into Strength

Insiders and institutions distributed quietly while retail bought aggressively.

f. The BL–SH Pattern Repeats

- Fear created the LOW zone (2018–2019).
- Euphoria created the HIGH zone (2020–2021).
- A crash reset the cycle (2022).

Tesla's mania proves that even the strongest companies follow predictable human cycles of fear and euphoria.

8.4 ITC Cycle

The ITC cycle is one of the clearest examples of how market sentiment, valuation compression, regulatory fear, and narrative shifts can suppress a fundamentally strong business for years — until the mispricing becomes too large to ignore. Then, almost suddenly, rerating happens and the stock delivers multi-year compounding.

This case study follows the four-part framework: **LOW Signal → HIGH Signal → What Happened → Lessons Learned**.

1. LOW Signal: 2014–2020 — "ITC is dead money."

For almost six years, ITC became a market joke. Despite being one of India's most profitable and diversified conglomerates, the stock went nowhere.

Sentiment Was Extremely Negative:

- "ITC is finished."
- "No one will touch tobacco stocks."
- "Zero growth. Zero returns."

Price Stagnation:

- ITC remained stuck between INR 200– INR 250 for years.
- Broader markets rallied drastically while ITC did not participate.
- Investors abandoned it for "high-growth" stories.

Narrative Overpowered Reality:

- Tobacco taxation fears dominated sentiment.
- ESG investors avoided "sin stocks."
- Analysts downgraded growth expectations harshly.

But Fundamentals Remained Strong:

- ITC's FMCG business grew steadily year after year.
- Operating margins improved.
- Cash reserves ballooned.
- Cigarettes remained a cash machine with 60–70% market share.
- Hotels, paper, and agri divisions contributed consistently.

Valuation Compressed to Irrational Levels:

- P/E compressed to 14–16×.

- Dividend yield crossed 4–5%.
- Free cash flow was extremely strong.

LOW-Zone Characteristics Present:

- Fear from regulatory news.
- Price far below intrinsic value.
- Strong fundamentals ignored.
- Long stagnation leading to capitulation.

ITC was a textbook LOW-zone opportunity created not by weakness — but by narrative pessimism.

2. HIGH Signal: 2021–2023 — The Rerating Wave

Once the undervaluation became too large, rerating began.

Price Breakout:

- ITC broke out of the INR 200– INR 250 range after years of sideways movement.
- The rerating accelerated sharply in 2022–2023.
- Stock rocketed to INR 450– INR 500+ levels.

Sentiment Flipped Completely:

- Media praised ITC's FMCG growth story.
- Analysts upgraded targets aggressively.
- Social media went from "ITC is dead" to "ITC to the moon."
- Retail investors flocked to the name.

Valuation Expanded:

- P/E rerated from 16× to 25–30×.
- Dividend yield compressed.
- Market priced in future FMCG dominance.

Signs of the HIGH Zone:

- Sharp momentum rallies.
- Massive retail participation.
- Viral memes ("ITC will never fall").

- Unrealistic projections for FMCG business.
- Brokerages issuing aggressive upgrades.

Smart Money Actions:

- Institutions trimmed around the peak.
- Early accumulation from 2016–2020 exited profitably.

This was not pure mania like Tesla or crypto, but it was a clear HIGH-zone rerating cycle driven by enthusiasm and stretched valuation.

3. What Happened: The Full ITC Cycle

2014–2020: Compression Phase

- Strong fundamentals.
- Weak sentiment.
- Flat price.

A multi-year LOW-zone opportunity for patient investors.

2021–2023: Expansion Phase

- Sentiment flipped rapidly.
- Price doubled over 18–24 months.
- Valuation expanded significantly.

2023–2024: Cooling Phase

- Valuation normalized.
- Price consolidated.
- Rerating peak completed.

Investors who bought during the LOW zone (range INR 200– INR 230) made multi-year compounding gains with extremely low risk.

4. Lessons Learned: ITC Proves the Power of Patience

- **Narratives can suppress price for years.** Even when fundamentals improve steadily.
- **Value compression creates spring-loaded upside.** When valuation becomes too low, rerating is inevitable.
- **Ranges create opportunity.** Long sideways markets are often signs of accumulation, not decay.

- **Sentiment flips faster than fundamentals.** One breakout changed a 6-year narrative.
- **The BL–SH cycle works in slow-motion too.** Not all cycles are fast or dramatic like crypto; some unfold over years.
- **Patience + valuation edge = massive asymmetric returns.**

ITC demonstrates that long-term stagnation is not death — it is often the start of a powerful rerating cycle.

8.5 PSU Banks Recovery

The recovery of India's PSU (Public Sector Undertaking) banks is one of the most dramatic "from despair to strong rerating" stories in Indian market history. For years, PSU banks were considered un-investable — burdened by NPAs, weak credit growth, governance doubts, and regulatory pressure. Then, almost quietly, fundamentals turned, valuations normalized, and a multi-year compounding cycle began.

This case study follows the four-part model: **LOW Signal → HIGH Signal → What Happened → Lessons Learned**.

1. LOW Signal: 2015–2020 — "PSU banks are finished."

For half a decade, PSU banks lived through extreme pessimism.

Sentiment Was Terrible:

- "PSU banks will never recover."
- "NPAs will destroy the system."
- "Only private banks will survive."
- "Government ownership means permanent underperformance."

Price Action:

- Stocks like SBI, Bank of Baroda, PNB, Canara, and Bank of India fell 60–90%.
- Nifty PSU Bank Index lost more than half its value.
- PSU banks massively underperformed private sector banks.

Macro + Policy Pressure:

- The NPA crisis exploded.
- Corporate defaults spiked.
- IBC (Insolvency and Bankruptcy Code) cases delayed resolutions.

- Provisioning requirements wiped out profits.
- Capital adequacy became a major concern.

But Fundamentals Quietly Improved Under the Surface:

- NPA recognition became more transparent.
- Provisioning buffers strengthened.
- Capital infusion by government stabilized balance sheets.
- Credit growth bottomed and slowly recovered.
- CASA ratios improved significantly.
- Cost-to-income ratios dropped.
- Digital transformation reduced inefficiencies.

Valuation Reached Ridiculous Levels:

- Many PSU banks traded at 0.3–0.6× book value.
- Market priced insolvency-level risks.
- Earnings forecasts assumed perpetual stagnation.

LOW-Zone Characteristics:

- Extreme fear and narrative pessimism.
- Price far below intrinsic (and book) value.
- Strong provisioning cycle laying foundation for recovery.
- High CASA, improving credit growth, stabilizing NPAs.
- No one willing to touch the sector.

This was one of the deepest, clearest LOW zones in Indian financial-sector history.

2. HIGH Signal: 2021–2023 — The Multi-Year Rerating Wave

Once stress cycles bottomed out, the PSU banking sector flipped rapidly.

Price Momentum Turned Strong:

- SBI surged from INR 150– INR 200 to INR 600+.
- Bank of Baroda tripled.
- Canara, Union, Indian Bank delivered 2–4× returns.

- Nifty PSU Bank Index became one of India's top-performing indices.

Sentiment Reversal:

- Analysts issued bullish notes for the first time in years.
- Retail investors returned aggressively.
- Media began highlighting "PSU Bank Revival Stories."
- Long-term bearish analysts flipped to optimistic forecasts.

Fundamentals Finally Understood:

- GNPA and NNPA fell sharply.
- Provision coverage ratios improved ¿80%.
- Credit growth rebounded strongly with economic recovery.
- Digital lending, UPI adoption, and efficiency gains boosted profitability.
- CASA and deposit franchise strengths were recognized again.

Valuation Expansion:

- P/B rerated from 0.4× to 1.2–1.8×.
- Market priced normalized profitability + growth.

Classic HIGH-Zone Signals Appear:

- Rapid price acceleration.
- Retail euphoria ("PSU banks will outperform forever").
- Broadcast media hype.
- Aggressive target upgrades based on optimistic credit cycles.

This was the HIGH-zone rerating phase — overconfidence replacing fear.

3. What Happened: The Full PSU Bank Cycle

Fear Phase (2015–2020):

- Sector abandoned by investors.
- Valuations near distress levels.
- Fundamentals slowly improving unnoticed.

Recovery Phase (2020–2021):

- NPAs peaked and began falling.

- Balance sheets stabilized.
- Loan growth returned.

Momentum Phase (2021–2022):

- Prices broke long-term ranges.
- Volumes surged.
- Re-rating began.

Euphoria Phase (2022–2023):

- Large multi-bagger returns in short time.
- Retail buying at the top.
- Analyst narratives turned overly optimistic.

Consolidation Phase (Post-2023):

- Prices cooled.
- Valuations normalized.
- Growth expectations stabilized.

Outcome:

- LOW-zone buyers (2018–2020) made 3–6× returns with low risk.
- MONEY made not because of prediction — but because of valuation + patience.
- Euphoria buyers faced corrections after the peak.

4. Lessons Learned: The PSU Bank Cycle Is a Masterclass in BL–SH

- **Undervaluation + improving fundamentals = explosive rerating potential.**
- **Narratives can keep price depressed long after fundamentals improve.**
- **Deep value opportunities often hide in hated sectors.**
- **Recovery cycles are multi-year and offer huge compounding.**
- **HIGH zones form quickly once sentiment flips.**
- **Most investors enter late — after the safe money has already been made.**

- **Markets overreact both ways: Fear pushes prices too low, Euphoria pushes them too high.**

The PSU bank recovery proves that even the most hated, ignored, and written-off sectors can become multi-baggers when fear peaks and fundamentals quietly strengthen.

8.6 RIL Cycle

Reliance Industries (RIL) is one of the most important case studies in Indian market history. It shows how a giant conglomerate can move through repeated LOW → HIGH cycles as it reinvents itself decade after decade. RIL's cycles demonstrate the power of transformation, sentiment reversals, and valuation waves driven by narrative, execution, and scale.

This case study follows the four-part model: **LOW Signal → HIGH Signal → What Happened → Lessons Learned**.

1. LOW Signal: 2012–2016 — "RIL is a dead stock."

Before RIL became India's most valuable company, it lived through years of stagnation.

Sentiment Was Weak:

- "Reliance has no growth left."
- "Legacy refining business will never rerate."
- "Telecom entry will destroy profits."
- "Conglomerate discount means permanent underperformance."

Price Action:

- RIL traded sideways for nearly 5 years.
- Stock remained stuck around INR 800– INR 1,000.
- The Nifty rallied strongly, but RIL lagged.

Narrative-Driven Negativity:

- Concerns around refining margins.
- Fear that massive capex would hurt balance sheet.
- Skepticism around Jio's viability.
- "Too big to grow" story spread widely.

But Fundamentals Quietly Strengthened:

- Petrochemicals margin improved.
- Retail operations expanded aggressively.
- Jio infrastructure rollout progressed at unprecedented speed.
- Balance sheet remained strong despite capex.

Valuation Became Ridiculously Low:

- P/E hovered around 10–12×.
- Market priced near-zero value for Jio and retail.
- Conglomerate discount ¿ 30–40%.

Clear LOW-Zone Indicators:

- Multi-year stagnation despite improving fundamentals.
- Valuation compression.
- Deep narrative pessimism.
- Capacity building ignored by the market.

This was one of the best large-cap LOW zones in Indian history.

2. HIGH Signal: 2017–2021 — The Jio & Retail Supercycle

Once Jio launched and scaled, everything flipped.

Price Acceleration:

- RIL surged from INR 1,000 to INR 2,000, then to INR 2,400+.
- Multiple rallies ¿50–100% happened in short spans.
- Market cap soared past $200 billion.

Sentiment Turned Hyper-Optimistic:

- "RIL will dominate telecom forever."
- "Jio is a monopoly."
- "Retail will surpass Amazon + Flipkart."
- "RIL is now a tech company."

Narrative Excess:

- Predictions of $1 trillion valuation.

- Assumptions of zero competition in telecom.
- Unrealistic retail market-share expectations.

Valuation Expanded Rapidly:

- P/E moved from 12× to 30–35×.
- Jio platform valuations soared.
- Global investors (Facebook, Google) invested at premium valuations.

Signs of the HIGH Zone:

- Parabolic upmoves.
- Massive retail participation.
- Media hype at all-time high.
- International institutions chasing the stock.
- Analysts raising targets every month.

Smart Money Behavior:

- Promoter stake reduction (rights issue, digital investments).
- Institutions booking partial profits.
- Business selling minority stakes at peak valuations.

This was a textbook HIGH-zone cluster: **euphoria + acceleration + narrative + extended valuation.**

3. What Happened: The Full RIL Cycle

Phase 1: Stagnation (2012–2016)

- Market ignored fundamentals.
- Valuation compressed.
- Heavy capex depressed sentiment.

Phase 2: Rerating & Momentum (2017–2019)

- Jio scale → sentiment flip.
- Stock broke multi-year range.
- Earnings visibility improved.

Phase 3: Mania (2020–2021)

- Multiple global tech giants invested.
- Retail and digital narrative peaked.
- Valuation reached euphoric levels.

Phase 4: Consolidation (2022–2023)

- Price stagnated around INR 2,200– INR 2,700.
- Valuations cooled.
- Market waited for next growth triggers (retail/Jio IPO).

Outcome:

- LOW-zone buyers (INR 800– INR 1,000 levels) made 2–3× safely.
- Momentum buyers made strong returns but faced volatility.
- Mania buyers (peak 2020–21) entered into a long sideways period.

4. Lessons Learned: The RIL Cycle Shows Multi-Layered BL–SH Dynamics

- **Conglomerates move through valuation cycles driven by narratives.** When narratives are negative, valuation compresses; when hype builds, valuation inflates.
- **Low valuation + strong future investments = powerful rerating potential.** The market ignored Jio's groundwork until it was too late.
- **Breakouts from long ranges often signal massive value unlock.** Once RIL broke past INR 1,100, the rerating accelerated.
- **Manias happen even in blue-chips.** Parabolic moves + extreme optimism = HIGH-zone signals.
- **Smart money sells into strength.** RIL's peak saw major stake sales to global investors at rich valuations.
- **Every cycle ends with cooling and consolidation.** No company — not even RIL — escapes valuation gravity.

RIL's cycle proves that even the strongest companies move through predictable fear → rerating → euphoria → consolidation patterns. The BL–SH System applies everywhere.

8.7 Midcap Boom–Bust Cycles

Midcaps are the heartbeat of Indian markets. They rise faster than large-caps during optimism and fall harder during panic. No segment demonstrates the BL–SH cycle more clearly, repeatedly, and violently than midcaps. Their boom–bust patterns offer some of the best opportunities for disciplined investors — and the biggest risks for emotional ones.

This case study follows the four-part model: **LOW Signal → HIGH Signal → What Happened → Lessons Learned.**

1. LOW Signal: Midcap Crashes (2013, 2016, 2018, 2020, 2022)

Midcap corrections happen with alarming regularity. Almost every 2–4 years, a major washout resets the entire segment.

Repeated LOW-Zone Characteristics:

- Prices fall 40–70% across the board.
- Institutional selling accelerates.
- Retail panic causes forced liquidation.
- Midcap indices underperform massively.
- Media declares midcaps "too risky" or "overvalued forever."

Examples of LOW Cycles:

2013 Crash

- Global volatility spike.
- Taper tantrum panic.
- Midcaps wiped out 40–60%.

2016 Correction

- Policy uncertainty.
- Earnings disappointments.
- Sharp midcap multiples compression.

2018–2019 Bloodbath

One of the worst midcap crashes in history:

- Many stocks fell 70–80%.
- Mutual fund reclassification triggered forced selling.
- Market narrative: "Midcaps are toxic."

2020 Covid Crash

- Index hit multi-year lows.
- Liquidity vanished.
- Best businesses sold at absurd discounts.

2022 Correction

- Inflation fears, global tightening.
- Midcap valuation reset once again.

Across all these cycles, one truth repeats:

Midcap LOW zones are created by fear, liquidity shock, and forced selling — not by the destruction of fundamentals.

2. HIGH Signal: Midcap Rallies (2014, 2017, 2021, 2023)

Midcap upcycles are equally explosive. Once risk appetite returns, midcaps often deliver 50–200% returns in short periods.

Repeated HIGH-Zone Characteristics:

- Rapid price acceleration across the entire segment.
- Retail participation surges dramatically.
- New demat accounts explode.
- Social media becomes extremely bullish.
- Analysts raise targets aggressively.
- Narratives like "midcaps = next multibaggers" dominate.

Examples of HIGH Cycles:

2014–2015 Bull Run

- India's macro turnaround.
- Midcaps doubled from 2013 lows.
- Valuations expanded rapidly.

2017 Mania

- One of the biggest midcap rallies this century.
- Many stocks gained 100–300%.
- P/E ratios reached extreme levels.

Classic HIGH signals were visible:

- Over-ownership in midcap mutual funds.
- Midcap IPO frenzy.
- Retail flooding into small-cap MFs.

2021–2023 Rerating

- Post-Covid recovery.
- Strong earnings.
- Multi-sector midcap outperformances.

In every cycle: Midcaps go from hated → loved → overbought → dangerous.

3. What Happened: The Boom–Bust Structure

Midcap cycles show the same predictable sequence:

Phase 1: Panic (LOW Zone)

- Sharp crashes.
- Forced mutual-fund selling.
- Liquidity disappears.
- Fundamentals ignored.

Phase 2: Early Recovery

- Institutions re-enter quietly.
- Earnings stabilize.
- Valuation remains deeply discounted.

Phase 3: Momentum Wave

- Prices break long-term resistance.
- Retail begins returning.

- Midcap index outperforms Nifty.

Phase 4: Euphoria (HIGH Zone)

- Parabolic price moves.
- Extreme overvaluation.
- Media hype and unrealistic projections.

Phase 5: Correction

- Valuation resets sharply.
- Weak businesses collapse.
- Strong businesses survive and compound again.

Outcome:

- Buying midcaps in LOW cycles produces 2–5× returns.
- Chasing midcaps in HIGH cycles usually leads to losses.
- Staying disciplined beats emotional timing.

4. Lessons Learned: Why Midcaps Are Perfect for BL–SH

- **Midcaps exaggerate every cycle.** Their volatility amplifies both fear (LOW) and euphoria (HIGH).
- **Most fear-driven crashes have nothing to do with fundamentals.** Liquidity, sentiment, and regulations drive panic selling.
- **Strong midcaps survive every crash and come back stronger.** Capital-efficient businesses multiply in each cycle.
- **Valuation matters more in midcaps than anywhere else.** Buying at LOW valuation is the only safe path.
- **Every midcap cycle creates new multibaggers — but only for disciplined buyers.**
- **Retail enters late, leaves early.** Emotional behavior creates predictable patterns of opportunity.
- **The BL–SH system works exceptionally well in midcaps** because the highs and lows are sharper, clearer, and more repeatable.

Midcaps are not unpredictable — they simply follow deeper, more dramatic BOOM → BUST → BOOM cycles. For disciplined investors, they are a compounding engine.

8.8 Netflix Cycles

Netflix is one of the clearest long-term examples of repeated LOW → HIGH → LOW cycles in a single company. The stock has experienced multiple expansions, corrections, and narrative reversals — often unrelated to the company's actual long-term fundamentals.

Studying Netflix reveals how narratives build, peak, break, and reset, making it one of the most important modern case studies for the BL–SH System.

1. The Early Growth Recovery Cycle (2012–2015)

The Fear: In 2011–2012, Netflix faced a major backlash due to:

- pricing missteps,
- subscriber churn,
- and skepticism about streaming viability.

The stock fell nearly 80%.

Why This Was a LOW Zone:

- Fundamentals were improving quietly.
- Streaming adoption accelerated globally.
- Content library expanded.
- Cash flow strengthened.

Narrative vs Reality: The market priced Netflix like a dying DVD company while it was becoming a global streaming giant.

Outcome: The stock went 15× from its lows over the next few years.

2. The Momentum → Euphoria Cycle (2016–2018)

This was one of the strongest HIGH zones in tech.

What Drove Euphoria:

- Explosive subscriber growth.
- Global expansion.
- Hit original shows (Stranger Things, Narcos).
- Analysts predicting "unlimited growth."

High-Zone Recognition Patterns:

- Parabolic price moves.

- Extreme valuation: P/E above 100.
- Narratives like "Netflix will replace all TV."
- Retail investors entering aggressively.
- Media celebrating subscriber growth every quarter.

Institutional Behavior: Large funds slowly began trimming positions into strength.

Outcome: Netflix corrected sharply multiple times in 2018–2019, resetting investor expectations.

3. The Pandemic Mania Cycle (2020–2021)

COVID lockdowns created one of Netflix's biggest demand surges ever.

The Mania Storyline:

- "Everyone is staying home — Netflix will grow forever."
- Streaming became an emotional safe haven.
- Subscriber numbers skyrocketed.

High-Zone Signals:

- Valuation stretched far above historical averages.
- Price accelerated rapidly.
- Retail investors bought heavily.
- Media ran stories of Netflix "owning entertainment."

What Everyone Missed:

- Demand was temporary (lockdown-driven).
- Competition from Disney+, Amazon Prime, HBO Max intensified.

Outcome: Netflix peaked around $700 and then began a massive correction.

4. The Crash Cycle (2022): One of the Biggest Large-Cap Resets

In 2022, Netflix fell more than 75% — one of the largest declines in a major global tech stock.

The Fear Narrative:

- Subscriber growth turned negative.

- Market believed saturation had arrived.
- Streaming competition pressures.
- Concerns over password sharing and slowing global expansion.

Why This Was a LOW Zone in Disguise:

- Fundamentals hadn't collapsed — they matured.
- Netflix remained the dominant global streaming brand.
- Cash-flow discipline improved dramatically.
- Advertising tier introduced — a huge monetization lever.

Valuation Reset:

- P/E compressed from 100+ to 20–25.
- Market priced Netflix like a no-growth utility.

This was a classic LOW zone: **panic-driven mispricing + healthy long-term fundamentals.**

5. The Recovery Cycle (2023–2024)

After the crash, Netflix stabilized and entered a steady recovery.

Drivers of Recovery:

- Reintroduction of disciplined content spending.
- crackdown on password sharing (led to subscriber surge),
- successful ad-supported plan,
- strong global franchises.

Sentiment Shift:

- From fear → cautious optimism → confidence.
- Analysts upgraded valuations steadily.

Outcome: Netflix rebounded impressively, proving once again that:

Value emerges when narrative breaks — not when narrative peaks.

Lessons from the Netflix Cycles

- **Narratives dominate Netflix more than fundamentals.**
- **Subscriber numbers create emotional overreactions.**
- **Parabolic growth always ends in correction.**
- **Deep sell-offs often reflect fear, not structural collapse.**
- **Netflix remains a cycle-driven stock — highly suited for BL–SH.**

Netflix teaches investors that even great businesses move through emotional extremes — and opportunity lies in recognizing the difference between fear and finality.

8.9 Nvidia 2018 and 2023

Few companies illustrate modern market cycles as dramatically as Nvidia. In just five years, Nvidia moved from a deep fear-driven LOW zone (2018) to one of the most powerful euphoria-driven HIGH zones of the decade (2023).

These two cycles show how rapidly sentiment, valuation, and narrative can flip — and how understanding the BL–SH structure allows investors to act rationally when the crowd loses perspective.

1. Nvidia 2018: The Fear Cycle (A Classic LOW Zone)

In late 2018, Nvidia suffered a 50–60% crash within months. This panic was driven not by long-term fundamentals collapsing, but by temporary, short-term narrative shocks.

What Triggered the Panic

- Crypto mining demand collapsed after the 2017 Bitcoin bubble burst.
- Inventory buildup in GPU channels led to oversupply.
- Market feared gaming demand would weaken.
- Global semiconductor slowdown hit headlines.
- Analysts predicted a multi-year stagnation.

Why The Fear Was Exaggerated

- Nvidia's core competitive advantage (GPU leadership) was intact.
- Gaming demand remained structurally strong.
- Data center and AI workloads were quietly accelerating.
- Margins remained robust despite temporary turbulence.

Valuation Reset → Opportunity

In the crash:

- Nvidia traded at one of its lowest P/E ratios in years.
- Price fell far below fair value.
- Sentiment turned extremely negative ("Nvidia is finished").

Classic LOW-Zone Indicators:

- Fundamentals intact
- Fear-driven selling
- Temporary shock (crypto-driven)
- Massive valuation discount
- Insiders and institutions quietly accumulating

Outcome

Within a year, Nvidia recovered aggressively. Within three years, Nvidia began one of the greatest runs in stock market history.

This cycle proved:

Temporary narrative collapses create generational buying zones.

—

2. Nvidia 2023: The AI Euphoria Cycle (A Strong HIGH Zone)

2023 marked Nvidia's transformation into the most discussed, most hyped, and most momentum-driven stock of the decade.

It became the centerpiece of the AI boom, fueled by ChatGPT, data center demand, and GPU shortages.

What Triggered the Mania

- Massive demand for AI compute.
- Companies rushing to build large GPU clusters.
- Nvidia's dominance in AI chips (A100, H100).
- Revenue guidance that shocked Wall Street.
- Media declaring "AI will change everything."

The Narrative Became Perfect

Investors believed:

- Every company will buy GPUs.
- Nvidia is the only AI chip provider.
- Demand will remain infinite.
- Margins will stay at record highs.

High-Zone Characteristics Clearly Visible

1. Extreme Valuation Stretch

- P/E expanded dramatically.
- Nvidia's market cap rose by trillions in months.

2. Parabolic Price Acceleration

- Multiple huge weekly green candles.
- No meaningful pullbacks.
- Straight-line rallies driven by FOMO.

3. Sentiment Euphoria

- Every tech headline featured AI.
- Social media overrun by Nvidia charts.
- Retail investors entered rapidly.
- Analysts competed to raise price targets.

4. Institutional Behavior

- Institutions trimmed exposure gradually.
- Insiders sold into strength.

- Hedge funds hedged aggressively.

5. Narrative Excess

- "Nvidia will be the first $10T company."
- "No other company can catch up."
- "AI will grow exponentially forever."

These are classic HIGH-zone markers — not signals of a bad company, but of an emotionally overheated market.

Why This Was a HIGH Zone

- Valuation disconnected from near-term fundamentals.
- Price acceleration outpaced revenue reality.
- Sentiment reached mania levels.
- New investors entered purely due to hype.

Outcome

Although Nvidia continued growing fundamentally, price experienced multiple sharp corrections and volatility spikes — typical after euphoric phases.

This cycle demonstrated:

Even world-class companies experience HIGH zones when narrative outruns fundamentals.

—

Key Lessons from Nvidia's 2018 and 2023 Cycles

- **Narratives create mispricing** — both on the downside and upside.
- **Temporary shocks create LOW zones** (2018).
- **Narrative perfection creates HIGH zones** (2023).
- **Fundamentals can remain strong even when price collapses.**
- **Valuation eventually normalizes after euphoria fades.**
- **The best opportunities often occur when fear is highest.**
- **The biggest risks occur when confidence is highest.**

Nvidia is the perfect teacher: fear creates entry, hype creates exit. Cycles repeat — even for the best companies on earth.

8.10 Meta: Collapse and Recovery

Meta (formerly Facebook) offers one of the most dramatic modern examples of how market sentiment can swing from absolute pessimism to renewed confidence. From 2022's historic crash to a stunning multi-year rebound, Meta shows the full Buy Low–Sell High cycle in action.

It is a masterclass in:

- fear-driven undervaluation,
- narrative collapse,
- structural resilience,
- disciplined turnaround,
- and re-rating based on fundamentals.

1. The 2021–2022 Breakdown: From Tech Giant to "Dying Company"

Meta's collapse was one of the steepest declines in mega-cap history. The stock fell nearly 75% from peak to trough — an unheard-of drop for a trillion-dollar company.

The Fear Narrative Took Over

A combination of events triggered widespread panic:

- Apple's privacy changes hit Meta's ad targeting model.
- TikTok surged, threatening user attention.
- Growth slowed after years of hyper-expansion.
- Heavy spending on the Metaverse sparked investor doubts.
- Media declared Meta's business model "broken."

Market Psychology:

- Investors priced Meta as if profits would permanently collapse.
- Analysts issued aggressive downgrades.
- Retail panic selling surged.

Valuation Collapse → LOW Zone Emerges

At the bottom:

- Meta traded at a single-digit P/E.
- Price fell far below fair value of the ad business.
- Multiple core products remained structurally strong.

LOW-Zone Signals Were Clear:

- Fundamentals intact (2–3 billion active users).
- Ad demand recovering with macro cycle.
- Unrealistic fear about "end of social media."
- Narrative overreaction, not structural breakdown.

It was a moment of maximum pessimism — and a generational accumulation opportunity.

—

2. The Turnaround Begins: Meta 2023

In 2023, Meta began one of the most impressive corporate turnarounds in modern history.

What Actually Changed

- Major cost cuts improved margins dramatically.
- Ad platform rebuilt around AI and first-party data.
- Reels competed effectively against TikTok.
- Metaverse spending rationalized and reduced.
- User growth returned across Instagram and WhatsApp.

Market Reaction

- Meta delivered shockingly strong income growth.
- Stock doubled, then tripled from lows.
- Analysts reversed their pessimism almost overnight.

Psychology Shift:

- Fear faded.

- Confidence returned.
- Long-term investors re-entered.

The LOW zone of 2022 became the launchpad for 2023's massive rally.

—

3. Meta's Full Recovery Cycle (2023–2024)

After stabilizing operations and cutting costs, Meta re-entered a maturity phase:

Drivers of Recovery:

- Advertising demand rebounded globally.
- Meta's AI-driven ad engine hit record efficiency.
- WhatsApp monetization began accelerating.
- Meta announced buybacks and capital discipline.
- Sentiment normalized from negative → optimistic.

Narrative Reversal:

- From "Meta is dying" to **"Meta is one of the strongest cash machines in tech."**

Valuation Re-Rating

As sentiment improved:

- P/E normalized.
- Market priced growth realistically.
- Institutions reallocated large capital.

Meta entered a new momentum phase — a textbook example of how fundamentals and sentiment reconnect after panic.

—

Lessons from the Meta Cycle

1. Sentiment can misprice even the strongest companies. Investors priced Meta as if its ad model was permanently destroyed — it wasn't.

2. LOW zones often appear when narratives break, not when fundamentals break.

3. Market pessimism magnifies short-term headwinds into dramatic stories.

4. The biggest opportunities emerge when investors overreact emotionally.

5. Meta's recovery shows how:

- business fundamentals,
- cost discipline,
- and large user ecosystems

can power enormous rebounds after fear-based selling.

6. Buy Low–Sell High works best when you recognize the difference between:

- temporary disruptions
- and true structural decline

Meta teaches a timeless truth: Narratives create collapses. Fundamentals create recoveries.

8.11 Housing 2020–2023

The global housing market during 2020–2023 is one of the most dramatic, emotionally driven, and misunderstood cycles of the modern era. It is a perfect example of how temporary shocks can create fear-driven LOW zones, followed by liquidity, demand surges, and eventual normalization.

This cycle demonstrates that even slow-moving asset classes such as real estate still follow the same BL–SH psychological pattern seen in stocks, crypto, and commodities.

1. The 2020 Shock: Panic, Uncertainty, and the Fastest LOW Zone in Property Markets

When COVID-19 spread globally in early 2020, housing markets faced unprecedented fear.

Why Panic Hit Hard:

- Full economic lockdowns halted mobility and home showings.
- Millions faced job loss or income uncertainty.
- Renters struggled to make payments.

- Headlines predicted "mass evictions," "40% price collapse," and "rental apocalypse."
- Investor sentiment turned deeply negative across all major cities.

Behavioral Response:

- Sellers reduced prices quickly to attract uncertain buyers.
- Investors paused purchases, waiting for "further crash."
- Retail panic led to distressed listings in many regions.

Why This Fear Was Temporary

Despite panic, long-term fundamentals did not break:

- Urbanization trends remained intact.
- Supply of quality housing was structurally low.
- Mortgage rates dropped to historic lows, boosting affordability.
- Government stimulus protected incomes and reduced distress.
- Institutional investors began quietly accumulating properties.

LOW-Zone Indicators Present:

- Sentiment extremely negative.
- Forced/distressed selling.
- Low transaction volume (fear freeze).
- Prices temporarily below intrinsic value.
- Strong fundamentals returning beneath the surface.

In many markets, home prices briefly discounted 10–20%, creating a stealth accumulation phase for long-term investors.

—

2. The 2021 Surge: From Fear to FOMO

As lockdowns eased, conditions shifted rapidly.

Drivers of the Rally

- Near-zero interest rates made mortgages historically cheap.
- Pent-up demand from delayed transactions.
- Remote work triggered relocation to larger or suburban homes.
- Investors sought inflation hedges and stable assets.
- Construction delays kept supply far below demand.

Result: A Housing Boom

- Prices surged 15–30% in many countries.
- Bidding wars became common.
- Homes sold above asking price within days.
- New buyers rushed in from FOMO.

Psychological Shift

- Fear disappeared.
- Confidence surged.
- Media declared a "new era" for housing.
- Social sentiment turned euphoric.

This phase represents the momentum + early euphoria stage of the cycle.

—

3. The 2022 Inflation Shock: Rates Rise, Sentiment Falls

By mid-2022, global inflation surged to multi-decade highs. To control it, central banks raised interest rates aggressively.

Impact on Housing:

- Mortgage rates doubled or tripled in some countries.
- Buyer affordability collapsed.
- Transaction volumes plummeted.
- Many first-time buyers were pushed out of the market.

Narrative Shift

- From "housing boom" → "housing bubble."
- Media predicted a "2008-style crash."
- Social sentiment turned highly pessimistic.

But Fundamentals Did Not Collapse:

- Housing supply remained historically low.
- Employment recovered fast.
- Institutional landlords held properties, limiting supply shocks.
- Most homeowners had fixed low-rate mortgages.

A New LOW Zone Began Forming:

- Prices softened but did not crash.
- Sellers offered discounts to serious buyers.
- Fear created opportunity for long-term investors.

—

4. The 2023 Normalization: Stability Returns

By 2023, housing markets entered a normalization phase.
Macro Environment Stabilized

- Inflation cooled slowly.
- Rate hikes paused or slowed.
- Economic activity stabilized globally.

Market Behavior:

- Prices stopped falling and began stabilizing.
- Transaction volumes increased slightly.
- Buyers returned cautiously.
- Builders resumed projects delayed since 2020.

Sentiment Normalization

- Fear eased but euphoria did not return.
- Social sentiment became "wait-and-watch."
- Investors selectively accumulated undervalued locations.

Outcome: Housing entered a balanced phase — not a boom or bust — with fundamentals and sentiment reconnecting after three years of extreme swings.

—

Lessons from the 2020–2023 Housing Cycle

- **Fear creates deep but temporary discounts** even in slow-moving markets.
- **Liquidity cycles drive real estate** just as strongly as financial markets.
- **Narratives change faster than fundamentals.**
- **Low supply and structural demand prevent long-term collapses.**
- **Euphoria leads to bidding wars, panic leads to opportunity.**
- **Normalization phases are where long-term compounding begins.**

Housing 2020–23 proves that even the most stable asset class still obeys the Buy Low–Sell High laws of cycles, emotion, and value.

8.12 Gold Cycles

Gold is unique among all major asset classes. It does not produce cash flows, does not depend on corporate earnings, and does not follow traditional valuation models.

Yet it moves in powerful, predictable cycles driven by:

- macroeconomic fear,
- inflation expectations,
- currency debasement,

- liquidity flows,
- and long-term sentiment swings.

Studying gold's cycles shows that even "safe-haven" assets experience deep LOW zones and powerful HIGH zones — all driven by human emotion, global uncertainty, and macro trends.

1. The 2008–2011 Supercycle: Crisis → Euphoria

Gold entered a massive cycle during the Global Financial Crisis.

2008–2009: The Fear-Driven LOW Zone

During the financial meltdown:

- Global markets collapsed.
- Trust in the banking system evaporated.
- Investors rushed toward safe assets.

Gold initially fell due to forced selling and liquidity needs, but fundamentals remained intact — **a classic LOW zone created by panic, not structural weakness.**

LOW-Zone Characteristics:

- Temporary liquidity stress.
- Long-term demand intact.
- Massive valuation discount relative to fear.

2010–2011: The Euphoria Peak

As the crisis progressed, gold entered a parabolic rally:

- Price surged from \$700 → \$1,900.
- Media declared "the end of fiat currency."
- Retail investors rushed to buy physical gold.
- Gold ETFs saw record inflows.
- Every correction was labeled a "buy."

HIGH-Zone Signals:

- Parabolic price acceleration.
- Extremely optimistic narratives.

- Crowd participation soared.
- Institutional selling increased.

Gold peaked in 2011 — **near the exact moment global fear peaked.**

—

2. The 2012–2015 Reset: From Euphoria to Deep Discount

After its 2011 highs, gold entered a multi-year corrective phase.

What Drove the Decline

- U.S. economic recovery.
- Strengthening dollar.
- Lower inflation fears.
- Reduced crisis-related demand.

Investor Psychology Shifted:

- From "gold only goes up" → "gold is dead."
- Retail investors exited.
- Media narratives turned negative.

LOW-Zone Characteristics (2015)

By 2015, gold:

- fell nearly 45% from its highs,
- traded near long-term support,
- was abandoned by retail investors,
- had no bullish media coverage.

Yet:

- global debt was rising,
- inflationary pressures were quietly building,
- supply growth slowed (mining costs increased).

This created one of the strongest *stealth accumulation phases* in gold's modern history.

—

3. The 2019–2020 Cycle: Inflation Meets Global Crisis

Gold entered a new cycle as macro conditions shifted.

2019: Early Momentum

Drivers:

- Falling interest rates.
- Concerns over global slowdown.
- U.S.–China trade tensions.

Momentum built steadily, but sentiment was still moderate — a healthy early-cycle phase.

2020: Panic → Mania

The COVID crisis triggered massive fear and global liquidity injections.
Gold surged sharply:

- Investors sought safe havens.
- Central banks printed record money.
- Negative real interest rates made gold highly attractive.

HIGH-Zone Traits:

- Gold hit an all-time high ($2,060).
- Media forecasted "$3,000–$5,000 gold."
- Retail flowed into gold ETFs at record speed.
- Sentiment reached euphoria.

This was the peak of a classic HIGH zone.
—

4. The 2021–2022 Pullback: Calm After Storm

Following the euphoria, gold moved into a consolidation phase.
What Changed:

- Economic reopening reduced safe-haven demand.
- Rising interest rates hurt gold's appeal.
- Liquidity contraction slowed flows into gold.

Psychology:

- Bullish narratives weakened.
- Retail interest dropped.
- Media attention vanished.

Outcome: Gold stabilized — not a crash, but a return to rational pricing. This set up the foundation for the next cycle.

—

5. The 2023 Cycle: Structural Demand + Quiet Rally

In 2023, gold began strengthening again — not due to panic this time, but due to structural demand and macro shifts.

Drivers of the Recovery

- Central banks (especially emerging markets) accumulated gold.
- Persistent inflation concerns.
- Geopolitical tensions boosted safe-haven demand.
- Dollar weakness re-emerged.

Psychological Condition:

- Sentiment was neutral, not euphoric.
- Media had low coverage.
- Retail investors were absent.

This created a low-noise accumulation environment — a sign of a healthy cycle base forming.

—

Lessons from Gold's Cycles

- **Gold booms when fear is high; cools when stability returns.**
- **LOW zones occur during periods of global calm and rising rates.**
- **HIGH zones occur during crises, inflation spikes, and liquidity waves.**
- **Narratives amplify emotions — both bullish and bearish.**
- **Central banks act as long-term accumulators, not speculators.**

- **Gold is cyclical, not linear — the BL–SH system applies perfectly.**

Gold teaches a timeless rule: Stability creates LOW zones, fear creates HIGH zones, and cycles repeat across generations.

8.13 Energy Cycles

The energy sector—especially oil and natural gas—moves through some of the most dramatic and predictable cycles in global markets. Unlike technology or consumer sectors, energy cycles are shaped by macroeconomic forces, geopolitical tensions, supply–demand imbalances, and large emotional swings.

From deep collapses to explosive bull runs, energy markets show how fear and scarcity create LOW and HIGH zones with extreme clarity. Understanding these cycles allows investors to apply Buy Low–Sell High with exceptional precision.

1. Understanding Energy Cyclicality

Energy prices are inherently cyclical because:

- Supply takes years to adjust (drilling, exploration, capital expenditure).
- Demand reacts instantly to economic growth or recession.
- Geopolitical events create large, sudden shocks.
- Inventories fluctuate based on global trade flows.
- Investor sentiment swings rapidly between scarcity and oversupply.

As a result:

- Oil and gas often overshoot on the upside during crises.
- They overshoot on the downside during recessions or gluts.

Energy cycles are a battle between structural fundamentals and emotional narratives.

—

2. The 2014–2016 Oil Collapse: A Textbook LOW Zone

The Shock:

- Global oil prices crashed from $110 to under $30.

- U.S. shale production surged unexpectedly.
- OPEC refused to cut output.
- Fears of long-term oversupply dominated the narrative.

Investor Psychology:

- Panic selling across energy equities.
- Media predicted "the end of high oil prices forever."
- Many believed electric vehicles would eliminate demand.

Why This Was a LOW Zone

- Demand remained strong globally.
- Fuel consumption kept rising in emerging markets.
- Shale output eventually slowed due to unprofitability.
- Capex (exploration & drilling) dropped sharply, ensuring future shortages.

Fundamentals vs Narrative: The world still needed massive amounts of energy, but the market priced oil companies as if global demand was collapsing permanently.

This mispricing created a deep accumulation opportunity.

—

3. The 2020 Crash: The Fastest and Deepest Energy LOW Zone in Modern History

COVID triggered one of the most extreme collapses ever seen in energy markets.

What Happened:

- Oil demand fell by more than 25%.
- Storage filled completely worldwide.
- Futures briefly went negative (WTI at -$37).
- Travel, aviation, and transportation shut down globally.

Investor Emotion:

- Pure panic.
- Headlines predicted "oil is worthless."
- Energy stocks were priced like they would all go bankrupt.

Why This Was an Extreme LOW Zone

- Energy demand was artificially suppressed, not structurally broken.
- Consumption began recovering within months.
- Low prices forced huge supply cuts.
- Capex collapsed, guaranteeing future shortages.

Long-term fundamentals remained intact, but prices fell to generational lows — textbook BL–SH opportunity.

—

4. The 2021–2022 Energy Supercycle: From Fear to Euphoria

As the world reopened, energy entered a powerful bull cycle.

Drivers of the Surge:

- Rapid rebound in global demand.
- Massive supply constraints from years of underinvestment.
- Geopolitical tensions (Russia–Ukraine crisis).
- OPEC maintaining tight production.
- Inventories falling rapidly.

Oil surged from negative levels in 2020 to over $120 in 2022.

HIGH-Zone Signals Appeared

- Extreme upward momentum.
- Retail investors rushing into energy stocks and ETFs.
- Media predicting "$200–$300 oil."
- Governments scrambling to control fuel inflation.

Narrative Euphoria:

- "Energy shortage is permanent."
- "Oil has entered a new golden age."
- "Demand will grow forever."

These are classic HIGH-zone markers — not because fundamentals were weak, but because sentiment became overheated.

—

5. The 2023–2024 Normalization: Post-Euphoria Cooling

After the 2021–2022 spike, energy markets cooled.

Why Prices Softened:

- Global growth slowed.
- Interest rates rose sharply.
- Strategic petroleum reserves (SPR) were released.
- Supply chains stabilized.

Psychological Shift:

- Euphoria faded.
- Fear disappeared.
- Sentiment became balanced and rational.

Outcome:

- Prices stabilized.
- Energy equities consolidated.
- Fundamentals reconnected with valuations.

This phase represents the reset portion of the energy cycle — the place where new LOW zones slowly begin forming.

—

Lessons from Energy Cycles

- **Panic creates undervaluation; scarcity creates euphoria.**
- **Energy cycles are driven by supply lag and demand shocks.**
- **Euphoria always collapses when supply catches up.**
- **LOW zones occur when everyone declares energy "dead."**
- **HIGH zones occur when headlines predict shortages forever.**
- **Investment booms sow the seeds of the next bust—and vice versa.**

Energy cycles prove that no asset is exempt from human emotion. Fear creates lows. Scarcity creates highs. And the cycle repeats endlessly.

Key Takeaways

- **The BL–SH cycle is universal across all assets.** From Amazon, Tesla, Meta, Nvidia, and Netflix to Bitcoin, gold, energy, ITC, PSU banks, and housing — every chart, every era, and every market shows the same emotional pattern: fear → accumulation → recovery → momentum → euphoria → correction → reset.

- **LOW zones always look terrifying in real time.** They are marked by panic headlines, collapsing sentiment, forced selling, extreme undervaluation, and narratives predicting permanent decline. Yet fundamentals are usually intact or improving beneath the surface.

- **HIGH zones always feel safe, justified, and "obvious."** Prices rise parabolically, optimism turns into certainty, valuation disconnects from reality, and investors believe the asset has achieved "escape velocity." This confidence is precisely what makes the zone dangerous.

- **Fundamentals strengthen long before the market acknowledges it.** In cycles like Meta, PSU banks, Nvidia, and Amazon, internal business recovery began months before price recovery — giving disciplined investors a massive edge.

- **Narratives drive mispricing far more than numbers.** Excess pessimism creates deep LOW zones (ITC, Meta 2022, Nvidia 2018, housing 2020). Excess optimism creates explosive HIGH zones (Tesla 2021, Bitcoin 2021, meme stocks, gold 2011).

- **Valuation amplifies human emotion.** Multiples collapse during fear and explode during euphoria, pushing prices far below fair value during panic and far above fair value during mania.

- **Smart money behaves opposite to retail.** Institutions and insiders accumulate quietly when fear dominates, and distribute quietly when retail excitement peaks. Understanding this flow is central to Buy Low–Sell High execution.

- **Cycles repeat regardless of sector, geography, or asset class.** Tech stocks, energy, commodities, crypto, midcaps, real estate — everything experiences boom–bust patterns because human psychology never changes.

- **Patience beats prediction.** The largest returns came not from forecasting news but from accumulating undervalued assets and holding them through the full cycle until euphoria.

- **You do not need to predict events — only recognize patterns.** LOW and HIGH signals appear with remarkable consistency: fear at bottoms, greed at tops, valuation extremes, narrative shifts, insider behavior, and sentiment changes.

- **The BL–SH System applies everywhere.** Whether it's Amazon, Bitcoin, ITC, midcaps, Meta, housing, gold, energy, or PSU banks — the same frameworks of value, sentiment, fundamentals, and narrative dynamics guide profitable decisions.

This chapter demonstrates one profound truth: **markets change, headlines change, technology changes — but human behavior never changes. And that makes Buy Low–Sell High timeless.**

Chapter 9

Risk Management for Normal People

Most people lose money in markets not because they misjudge valuation, timing, or fundamentals — but because they underestimate risk.

Risk is invisible when things are going well and brutally real when things go wrong.

This chapter teaches a complete, practical, simple system for normal people — not traders, not quants, not hedge funds — to survive volatility, avoid catastrophic mistakes, and ensure that Buy Low–Sell High actually works over decades.

Risk management is not optional. It is the single biggest reason why some investors survive every cycle while others blow up after one bad year.

Why Risk Management Matters

Before learning how to manage risk, remember one universal rule:

You cannot compound if you cannot survive.

If you lose:

$$-50\% \rightarrow \text{you need } +100\% \text{ to recover}$$

$$-80\% \rightarrow \text{you need } +400\% \text{ to recover}$$

Most people never recover large drawdowns because they run out of:

- time,
- capital,

- or emotional confidence.

This chapter prevents that outcome.

—

9.1 Hedging: Protection When Things Break

You don't need to hedge every day — you hedge when:

- valuations are stretched,
- sentiment is euphoric,
- you have large unrealized profits,
- macro risks are rising,
- liquidity is tightening.

Simple Hedging Methods for Normal People

1. Index ETFs as Hedge Exposure Buy small positions in inverse index ETFs when markets enter HIGH zones. A 5–10% hedge often protects 30–40% of portfolio risk.

2. Cash Hedge Holding 10–30% cash during euphoric phases is a valid hedge. Cash is an option — it gives you the power to buy when others panic.

3. Sector Rotation Hedge Move part of your portfolio into:

- defensives (FMCG, utilities),
- gold,
- short-duration bonds,

when markets overheat.

When NOT to Hedge

- In deep LOW zones — panic hedging is a disaster.
- When volatility is high and expensive.
- When fundamentals are strong and fear-driven declines create opportunity.

Hedging is insurance — use it when the house is uncomfortably hot, not when it's already burning.

—

9.2 Stop-Loss Logic: Mechanical, Not Emotional

Stop-losses are not for predicting crashes. They are for preventing one bad position from destroying your future.

Rules for Effective Stop-Losses

1. Never Put Stop-Losses on Long-Term Value Positions LOW-zone entries should not be auto-sold due to volatility.

2. Always Use Stop-Losses on High-Zone Momentum Positions If you bought something in late momentum or early euphoria, you must protect yourself.

3. Use Trailing Stops for Winners A trailing stop locks in profit while allowing upside.

4. Stop-Loss Range Use:

- 8–12% for short-term trades,
- 15–25% for cyclical positions,
- volatility-adjusted stops for commodity/crypto.

5. Never Widen a Stop This is how disasters begin.

6. Never Ignore a Stop If your system says exit — you exit.

—

9.3 Portfolio Construction: Build for Survival First

Your portfolio should be built around:

- stability,
- diversification,
- risk parity,
- and clarity of purpose.

The 3-Bucket Framework

Bucket 1: Core (50–70%) Large caps, indices, high-quality businesses. This is your compounding engine.

Bucket 2: Cyclical / Value (20–40%) LOW-zone opportunities:

- PSU banks,

- ITC-type cases,
- high-quality midcaps after crashes,
- commodities after down-cycles.

Bucket 3: High-Volatility (5–15% max) Crypto, smallcaps, momentum plays. This bucket should **never** threaten your financial survival.

Rules for Construction

1. No single stock ¿ 10% of portfolio (unless Core).
2. No single high-volatility asset ¿ 3–5%.
3. Limit correlated positions. Owning 5 tech stocks is not diversification.
4. Maintain liquidity buffer. 10–20% cash gives you firepower during LOW zones.

—

9.4 Asset Allocation Templates

Different people need different allocation setups.

1. Conservative Allocation

- 60% Equity (large-cap + index)
- 20% Bonds
- 10% Gold
- 10% Cash

2. Balanced Allocation

- 70% Equity
- 10% Bonds
- 10% Gold
- 10% Cash

3. Aggressive Allocation

- 70–80% Equity
- 10% Gold
- 10–20% Cash for LOW-zone buying

4. Cycle-Based Allocation (BL–SH Optimized)

In LOW zones:

- Increase equity exposure (70–90%)
- Reduce bonds/cash
- Increase cyclicals

In HIGH zones:

- Increase cash (20–40%)
- Increase bonds/gold
- Reduce equity exposure

Markets are cyclical; your allocation should be dynamic, not dogmatic.

—

9.5 Drawdown Math: The Truth No One Wants to Accept

The deeper your loss, the harder recovery becomes.

Loss	Required Gain
-10%	+11%
-20%	+25%
-30%	+43%
-40%	+67%
-50%	+100%
-60%	+150%
-70%	+233%
-80%	+400%

This is why:

- risk controls are mandatory,
- diversification matters,
- oversized positions destroy portfolios,
- drawdown avoidance is more important than chasing returns.

Wealth compounds only when drawdowns stay small and survivable.

—

9.6 Position Sizing Rules (Advanced)

Sizing determines your fate more than stock selection.

1. The 1–2–5 Rule

- 1% risk per trade (high volatility)
- 2% risk per cyclical play
- 5% max for high-conviction positions

2. Volatility-Based Sizing

Risk less on:

- smallcaps,
- commodities,
- crypto,
- unproven stories.

Risk more on:

- index funds,
- established blue chips.

3. The 50% Rule

No single sector should exceed 50% of your portfolio (except index-based, broad-market funds).

4. Scaling Into LOW Zones

Use:

- 30% initial,
- 30% if valuation stays low,
- 40% on momentum reversal.

This prevents emotional all-in buying.

—

9.7 How to Not Blow Up: Survival Rules

1. Never Go All-In

Even if you are "sure," you are still vulnerable to:

- black swan events,
- liquidity shocks,
- macro surprises,
- regulatory changes.

2. Avoid Leverage for Long-Term Investing

Leverage accelerates returns only during uptrends; it destroys you during corrections.

3. Beware of Correlated Bets

Tech stocks, crypto tokens, or energy equities tend to crash together.

4. Avoid Emotional Averaging Down

Averaging down only works in LOW zones — not in failing businesses.

5. Always Keep a Cash Buffer

Cash = survival + opportunity.

—

9.8 Death-Spiral Avoidance Framework

A "death spiral" is when:

- your losses reduce your confidence,
- your reduced confidence leads to bad decisions,
- bad decisions cause further losses.

To escape:

1. Stop Trading Immediately

Pause. Reset. Think.

2. Review the Decision Journal

Identify:

- what triggered impulsive decisions,
- what emotional state you were in,
- what rule you violated.

3. Reduce Position Size by 50–70% Temporarily

Shrink risk until discipline returns.

4. Move Back to Your System

Emotion → system → discipline → stability.

5. Rebuild Slowly

Once stable, rebuild exposure gradually — never instantly.

—

Final Message

Risk management is the unseen engine behind every great investor's success. You do not win by being brave — you win by being disciplined.

Your #1 job is survival. Your #2 job is compounding. Everything else is optional.

Key Takeaways

- **Survival is the foundation of compounding.** You cannot build wealth if a single mistake destroys your capital. Risk management protects the long-term compounding engine.
- **Risk is invisible during bull markets and obvious during crashes.** The time to prepare is before volatility arrives, not after.
- **Hedging is insurance, not speculation.** Small hedges, cash buffers, and defensive allocation dramatically reduce portfolio drawdowns during HIGH zones.
- **Stop-losses are mechanical protection, not emotional decisions.** Use them on momentum positions and speculation; avoid them on long-term LOW-zone value buys.

- **Position sizing determines your destiny.** Even good ideas fail if sized too large; even average ideas succeed if sized correctly. The goal is to avoid any single position harming the portfolio.
- **Diversification prevents catastrophic loss.** Spread risk across sectors, factors, and asset classes. Avoid heavy concentration in correlated bets.
- **Healthy portfolios use a bucket system.** Core → Value/Cyclical → High Volatility. Clear roles prevent emotional allocation mistakes.
- **Asset allocation should be dynamic, not fixed.** Increase risk during LOW zones, decrease risk during HIGH zones. This turns cycles into opportunity instead of danger.
- **Deep drawdowns destroy compounding speed.** A 50% loss requires +100% to recover. Avoiding big losses is mathematically more powerful than chasing returns.
- **Cash is not "dead money" — it is optionality.** Cash is what lets you buy assets during fear instead of watching opportunity pass by.
- **Never widen a stop, never add blindly, never go all-in.** These are the three behaviors that trigger financial death spirals.
- **The death-spiral avoidance framework breaks emotional loops.** Pause → Journal → Reduce size → Return to system → Rebuild slowly. This is how normal investors prevent permanent damage.
- **Risk management is a habit, not a tool.** It must be practiced every month, not activated only when things go wrong.

In the end: Risk management does not limit your upside — it protects your ability to stay in the game long enough to let Buy Low–Sell High work its magic.

Chapter 10

Building a Millionaire Portfolio

A system is only valuable if it can be executed. This chapter shows how to use the Buy Low–Sell High framework to build a portfolio capable of compounding to millionaire-level wealth over 10–20–30 year horizons.

You will learn:

- how to structure portfolios at different capital sizes,
- how to allocate across cycles,
- how to rotate during bull and bear markets,
- how beginners differ from advanced investors,
- and how to follow a long-term roadmap that guarantees survival and growth.

This chapter turns the entire book into a real-life wealth strategy.

10.1 The Goal: A Portfolio That Compounds in Every Market

Most investors build portfolios that work only in good times. A millionaire portfolio must:

- survive crashes,
- grow during expansions,
- rotate during cycles,

- and accumulate aggressively in LOW zones.

We are not trying to get rich quickly. We are trying to get rich permanently.

The BL–SH system gives you the ability to:

- buy assets when they are undervalued,
- hold them until valuation and sentiment peak,
- exit methodically,
- and repeat the process across decades.

This is how millionaires are built.

—

10.2 Sample Portfolios: From $10k to $500k

These examples show how to structure capital to maximize survival and long-term compounding.

1. The $10,000 Portfolio (Beginner Level)

Goal: Learning, discipline, risk control.

Suggested Allocation:

- 50% Index Funds / ETFs (core stability)
- 20% Large-cap value (PSU banks, ITC-type cases)
- 15% High-quality midcaps
- 10% Cash (for LOW-zone buys)
- 5% Crypto / High-volatility assets

Why this works:

- High diversification
- Low risk of ruin
- Simple to manage
- Perfect for learning the BL–SH cycle behavior

—

2. The $50,000 Portfolio (Growing Investor)

Goal: Stronger cyclicality, more targeted opportunities.

Suggested Allocation:

- 40% Index + High-quality large caps
- 25% Cyclical/value buys (LOW zones)
- 20% Midcaps with strong fundamentals
- 10% Cash
- 5% Crypto or commodity cycle exposure

Why this works:

- Enables larger LOW-zone entries
- Smooths volatility through core holdings
- Maintains optionality through cash

—

3. The $100,000 Portfolio (Compounding Mode)

Goal: Systematic cycle rotation + scaling.

Suggested Allocation:

- 35% Index + Blue chips
- 30% Value picks (PSU banks, old-economy winners)
- 20% Midcaps bought during corrections
- 10% Sector rotation (energy/gold cycles)
- 5% Cash reserve

Why this works:

- Capital begins compounding visibly
- LOW-zone cycles generate meaningful returns
- Portfolio can swallow volatility without panic

—

4. The $500,000 Portfolio (Serious Wealth Builder)

Goal: Capital protection + strong cyclical upside + tax efficiency.

Suggested Allocation:

- 40% Global + Domestic Index Funds (risk anchor)
- 25% Large-cap value and cyclicals (LOW zones)
- 20% Midcaps/Smallcaps with filters
- 10% Gold/Energy/Commodities (hedge + cycle)
- 5% Opportunistic cash or hedging

Why this works:

- Stability prevents major drawdowns
- Exposure to cyclical upside creates alpha
- Global diversification protects long-term wealth

This structure is capable of compounding into million-dollar territory if cycle discipline is maintained.

—

10.3 Rules for Beginners vs Advanced Investors

Beginners

- Avoid high concentration.
- Avoid leverage.
- Don't chase momentum.
- Focus on index + value.
- Learn cycle signals before acting big.

Advanced Investors

- Increase cyclical allocation during LOW zones.
- Use sector rotation across cycles (energy, metals, tech).
- Use trailing stops during euphoric phases.
- Hedge selectively during HIGH zones.
- Size positions based on volatility and conviction.

Advanced investors earn more not because they predict better — but because they survive better and rotate better.

—

10.4 Long-Term Roadmap: 5–10–20–30 Years

Years 1–5: Foundation Stage

- Build index-heavy portfolio.
- Practice LOW-zone identification.
- Learn emotional discipline.
- Avoid oversized risks.

Years 5–10: Scaling Stage

- Increase exposure to value and midcaps.
- Implement cycle-based entries and exits.
- Build cash reserves for opportunities.
- Optimize taxes and global diversification.

Years 10–20: Compounding Stage

- Portfolio starts snowballing.
- Rotate across cycles with confidence.
- Reduce speculation; increase quality.
- Maintain strict risk management.

Years 20–30: Freedom Stage

- Shift toward stability (index + defensive sectors).
- Reduce volatility exposure.
- Preserve capital for generational wealth.

This roadmap aligns with how real millionaires are built — through stability, cycles, and discipline.

—

10.5 How to Rotate Across Cycles

Cycle rotation is the secret weapon of the BL–SH strategy.

In LOW Zones (Fear Phase)

- Increase equity allocation.
- Accumulate high-quality cyclicals.
- Deploy cash strategically.

In Momentum Zones

- Hold strong positions.
- Reduce exposure to weak assets.
- Begin preparing exit levels.

In HIGH Zones (Euphoria Phase)

- Scale out 25–50%.
- Hedge selectively.
- Raise cash levels.

In Recession/Panic Phases

- Avoid rushing.
- Watch for fundamental strength.
- Prepare for the next accumulation wave.

Rotation = The art of moving capital where the opportunity is newest and safest.

—

10.6 How to Survive Bear Markets

Survival determines whether you become wealthy or not.

Never Do These in Bear Markets

- Do not panic sell due to fear.
- Do not average down blindly.
- Do not hold overvalued assets hoping they recover.

Always Do These

- Hold high-quality businesses (they recover).
- Keep cash — it is your weapon.
- Avoid leverage completely.
- Add only when fundamentals stay intact.
- Use dollar-cost accumulation in LOW zones.

Bear markets create millionaires not by breakout trades but by disciplined accumulation.

—

Final Message

Becoming a millionaire is not about genius, luck, or insider information. It is about:

- surviving drawdowns,
- buying during fear,
- selling during euphoria,
- managing risk intelligently,
- and repeating the cycle for decades.

Wealth is built by systems, not emotions. The BL–SH framework is that system.

Key Takeaways

- **Millionaire wealth is built through cycles, not single trades.** The investors who consistently buy LOW and sell HIGH over decades accumulate far more wealth than those chasing short-term moves.
- **Portfolio size does not matter — discipline does.** Whether you start with $10k or $500k, the BL–SH structure allows steady, long-term compounding.
- **Core stability + cyclical opportunities = optimal growth.** Index funds and blue chips provide the foundation. LOW-zone cyclicals provide the acceleration.

- **Cash is a strategic weapon.** Holding 5–20% cash allows you to strike during fear-driven LOW zones instead of watching opportunity pass by.
- **Beginners must focus on safety; advanced investors focus on rotation.** Beginners avoid leverage, concentration, and momentum chasing. Advanced investors use hedging, sizing, and cycle rotation.
- **Asset allocation must change with the cycle.** Increase equity exposure in fear phases. Increase cash and defensives in euphoric phases. Portfolios should be dynamic — not fixed.
- **Bear markets are not threats — they are where millionaires are made.** Crashes create undervaluation, panic discounts, and generational buying windows. Survivors accumulate; emotional investors capitulate.
- **Long-term wealth comes from consistency, not predictions.** Following the roadmap for 5–10–20–30 years delivers far more wealth than trying to time micro-movements.
- **No single position should ever threaten your financial survival.** Proper position sizing ensures that even wrong decisions cannot destroy the portfolio.
- **The system works at every capital level.** $10k portfolios learn discipline. $50k portfolios build structure. $100k portfolios scale. $500k portfolios compound into millionaire territory.
- **Cycle rotation is the secret to superior returns.** Move capital:
  - into fear (accumulation),
  - through recovery (hold),
  - out of euphoria (scale-out),
  - and wait for the next reset.
- **Becoming a millionaire is a system, not a dream.** With risk management + cycle discipline + long-term allocation, the outcome becomes a mathematical inevitability.

Final insight: A millionaire portfolio is not built by luck or brilliance — it is built by a repeatable process applied patiently over time.

Chapter 11

The Wealth Equation

Every great investor eventually discovers one truth: wealth is not built by prediction, luck, or intelligence — it is built by a simple, repeatable mathematical law.

$$\textbf{Wealth} = (\textbf{Capital} \times \textbf{Accuracy} \times \textbf{Cycles Repeated})$$

This chapter introduces the universal equation behind long-term compounding. It explains why you don't need to win every trade, time every top, or avoid every correction. You only need three things:

- **Capital** — deployed consistently, not emotionally.
- **Accuracy** — a system that identifies LOW zones and HIGH zones.
- **Cycles Repeated** — the discipline to repeat the process.

Wealth grows when these three components multiply. The more cycles you repeat with accuracy, the more your capital compounds.

This chapter shows how simple, mechanical decisions — applied again and again — produce exponential results over time.

11.1 The Universal Compounding Law

Every long-term wealth creator—across every market, country, and era—follows the same mathematical law, whether consciously or unconsciously. It is the engine behind all exponential results:

$$\textbf{Wealth} = (\textbf{Capital} \times \textbf{Accuracy} \times \textbf{Cycles Repeated})$$

This equation is simple, but it explains everything: why wealth concentrates in the hands of disciplined investors, why emotional investors underperform, and why even average accuracy becomes extraordinary when repeated across cycles.

This section breaks the equation into its three essential components and shows how they multiply to create long-term compounding.

1. Capital — The Foundation of Growth

Capital is the starting fuel for compounding. The more capital you deploy with discipline, the more powerful the equation becomes. But capital alone does not create wealth—how and when you allocate it matters.

Capital grows through:

- consistent saving,
- avoiding big losses,
- reinvesting profits,
- upgrading skills and income,
- resisting emotional trades that destroy principal.

Capital is your base multiplier. Even small improvements in capital—5–10% more saved each year—become massive over multiple cycles.

But the equation does not stop here. Without accuracy and repetition, capital remains stagnant.

2. Accuracy — The System That Tilts the Odds

Accuracy does not mean perfection. It does not mean timing every bottom or selling the exact top. It means having a structured method—like the BL–SH framework—that consistently positions you on the right side of probability.

Accuracy increases when you:

- buy in LOW zones (fear, undervaluation, strong fundamentals),
- avoid emotional buying in HIGH zones,
- sell into strength instead of panic,
- use rules, checklists, and predefined exit levels,
- maintain a system-driven approach.

With even **60–70% accuracy**, your wealth curve becomes exponential. You do not need 90% accuracy. You only need slightly better decisions than the crowd—repeated consistently.

This is the hidden truth: You don't need to win every time. You only need to win more often than you lose, and avoid catastrophic errors.

3. Cycles Repeated — The Hidden Exponential Multiplier

This is where true wealth comes from. Not from a single great investment. Not from one lucky year. But from repeating the right cycle many times.

A single successful LOW → HIGH cycle is useful. Ten cycles are life-changing.

Cycles repeated means:

- buying undervalued assets again and again,
- selling overvalued assets again and again,
- surviving corrections so you can reinvest,
- staying invested long enough for compounding to matter.

The majority of investors fail not because of bad choices, but because they stop the cycle:

- they panic during crashes,
- chase euphoria at tops,
- trade emotionally,
- break the process halfway.

Repetition is the true exponent in the equation. The more cycles you complete, the faster capital grows—even with average accuracy.

4. You Don't Need to Win Every Time

This is the psychological breakthrough most investors never achieve.

You do not need:

- perfect timing,
- magical predictions,
- zero losses,
- constant trading.

You only need:

- a system that is directionally correct,
- protection against large losses,
- consistent participation in cycles.

Even a method that is right **slightly more often than wrong**, when repeated across many cycles, generates extraordinary wealth.

The key is survival + repetition. Not prediction + perfection.

5. Wealth Is Mechanical, Not Emotional

Most investors treat wealth as an emotional journey. But true wealth follows mathematics, not mood.

The Wealth Equation does not care if you:

- feel fearful today,
- feel excited tomorrow,
- read positive or negative news,
- are surrounded by hype or panic.

Markets reward:

- structure,
- patience,
- process,
- and repetition.

Emotion destroys compounding. Mechanics protect it.

Wealth is not the result of how you feel — it is the result of what you repeat.

The Wealth Equation turns investing into a predictable engine. Once you understand how Capital, Accuracy, and Cycles multiply, you no longer chase luck. You build wealth mechanically.

Chapter 12

The One-Page Master Summary

Every great system needs a simple dashboard — a single, clear page you can return to before every decision. This chapter compresses the entire BL–SH Method into one practical, screenshot-ready master summary. It gives you the buy rules, the sell rules, the definitions of LOW and HIGH, the full BL–SH 7-Step System, and a mini checklist that you can use for life.

This is the page that converts theory into practice, and practice into results.

1. Buy Rules (The LOW-Zone Playbook)

You buy when the market is fearful, valuation is discounted, and fundamentals remain solid. The LOW zone is defined by mispricing caused by emotion — not permanent damage.

Buy Only When:

- Price is 20–70% below fair value.
- Fundamentals are intact: revenue stable, debt manageable, margins stable or improving.
- The sell-off is driven by fear, panic, or macro noise — not structural collapse.
- Sentiment is negative or indifferent; headlines are pessimistic.
- High-quality insiders or institutions are accumulating.
- Price is near long-term support or capitulation levels.
- Narrative is negative but facts contradict the fear.

If fear feels high and narrative feels hopeless — you are close to the LOW zone.

2. Sell Rules (The HIGH-Zone Playbook)

You sell when the market gets euphoric, valuation stretches, and price accelerates unsustainably. The HIGH zone is defined by emotional excess, not fundamental strength.

Sell or Trim When:

- Price trades above your fair-value upper range.
- Valuation is stretched relative to history and peers.
- Price goes parabolic — straight upward acceleration.
- Mainstream media is consistently bullish.
- New retail investors rush in late out of FOMO.
- Insider selling increases; institutions quietly distribute.
- Narratives shift to "This time it's different."

If everything feels easy, safe, and obvious — you are near the HIGH zone.

3. What "LOW" Really Means

A LOW zone is not just a low price — it is a combination of value, fear, and opportunity.

The Definition of LOW:

LOW = Strong Fundamentals + Temporary Fear + Valuation Discount

LOW-Zone Conditions:

- Asset trades far below intrinsic value.
- Long-term business or macro engine unchanged.
- Panic-driven sell-off forces price down.
- Sentiment is extremely negative.
- Investors overreact to temporary setbacks.

LOW zones feel uncomfortable — which is exactly why they work.

4. What "HIGH" Really Means

A HIGH zone is not merely a high price — it is a psychological peak supported by euphoria and excess.

The Definition of HIGH:

$$\textbf{HIGH} = \textbf{Overvaluation} + \textbf{Mania} + \textbf{Narrative Excess}$$

HIGH-Zone Conditions:

- Price far above intrinsic value.
- Crowd believes the asset is a "sure thing."
- Narrative becomes unrealistic or perfect.
- Price rises faster than fundamentals.
- New beginners enter aggressively at the top.

HIGH zones feel safe — which is why they are dangerous.

5. The BL–SH 7-Step System (The Full Execution Method)

This is your operating system — the entire BL–SH Method reduced to the seven actions you repeat forever.

1. **Scan for undervalued assets** Use PE, PB, FCF, RSI, volatility indices, and macro context.
2. **Validate fundamentals** Revenue, debt, cash flow, moat, management, long-term demand.
3. **Estimate fair value** Use simple, repeatable models — not complex forecasting.
4. **Enter in the LOW Zone** Only buy when price ¡ fair value with fear-driven mispricing.
5. **Set HIGH-zone exit targets** Predetermine your exit levels before you enter.
6. **Scale-out profits** Take partial profits (25–50%) at fair value; let the remaining portion ride with trailing stops.
7. **Repeat the cycle** This repetition is where compounding becomes exponential.

The 7-Step System is your compass in every market condition.

6. The Screenshot-Ready Mini Checklist

A one-page checklist you can refer to before every buy or sell:

BUY Checklist (LOW Zone)	**SELL Checklist (HIGH Zone)**
Price 20–70% below fair value	Price above upper fair-value bound
Fundamentals intact	Valuation stretched
Fear-driven sell-off	Parabolic price rise
Negative sentiment, scary headlines	Euphoria, extreme optimism
Institutional/insider buying	Insider selling, institutional distribution
Strong long-term story unchanged	"This time it's different" narratives

If the left column dominates → Buy. If the right column dominates → Sell.

This single page gives you:

- clarity,
- confidence,
- emotional neutrality,
- and consistent execution.

This summary is your compass for every market cycle — the core of the BL–SH Method in one powerful page.

Part I

Appendix

Glossary

Accumulation A phase where smart money quietly buys undervalued assets during fear and low sentiment.

Accuracy The reliability of your investment decisions. In the BL–SH System, accuracy means consistently identifying LOW zones for buying and HIGH zones for selling.

Bear Market A prolonged period of falling prices, negative sentiment, and heightened fear. Often produces LOW-zone opportunities.

Bottom The price point at or near the end of a downtrend, typically marked by panic selling, capitulation, and extreme undervaluation.

Buy Low–Sell High (BL–SH) The core strategy of buying assets when they are undervalued and selling when they become overpriced due to euphoria.

Capital The money you deploy to invest. One of the three multipliers in the Wealth Equation.

Cycles Repeated market phases such as fear, recovery, momentum, euphoria, and correction. Compounding occurs by repeating cycles consistently.

Distribution A phase where smart money sells portions of their holdings to retail investors during euphoria.

Euphoria An emotional market state where asset prices surge rapidly due to extreme optimism. A key HIGH-zone indicator.

Fair Value An estimate of an asset's true worth based on fundamentals. Buying below fair value increases long-term returns.

Fear Zone A period marked by panic, negative headlines, and undervalued prices — ideal for accumulation.

Fundamentals The underlying business drivers such as revenue, margins, cash flow, debt, and competitive advantage.

High Zone A phase where price exceeds fair value due to overconfidence, mania, and narrative excess.

Intrinsic Value The true economic value of an asset based on its ability to generate future cash flows.

Liquidity Shock A sudden withdrawal of buyers or capital, causing rapid price drops — often creating LOW zones.

Low Zone The accumulation-friendly phase characterized by undervaluation, fear, and intact fundamentals.

Momentum Phase A period where price begins rising steadily after a bottom, with increasing participation and confidence.

Narrative The story the market tells about an asset. Narratives drive mispricing in both LOW and HIGH zones.

Overvaluation A condition where price trades significantly above intrinsic value due to hype or excessive optimism.

Parabolic Move A sharp, unsustainable, vertical price increase that often precedes a peak.

Price Acceleration Rapid upward movement in the market, often caused by FOMO, bullish speculation, or momentum chasing.

Recency Bias A cognitive bias where investors assume recent events will continue indefinitely.

Rerating A sustained increase in valuation multiples when fundamentals or sentiment improve.

Risk Management A set of rules that protect capital from large losses — an essential part of the BL–SH System.

Sentiment The emotional state of the market: fear, neutrality, or euphoria. Drives short-term mispricing.

Smart Money Experienced investors, institutions, or insiders who accumulate quietly during fear and sell into strength.

Support Zone A price area where buyers historically enter, reducing downside pressure.

System A rule-based, repeatable method for making decisions. The BL–SH System replaces emotional decision-making.

Trailing Stop A dynamic exit tool that locks in profits as price rises while protecting against reversals.

Valuation The process of determining an asset's worth using metrics such as PE, PB, EV/EBITDA, and FCF yield.

Volatility The degree of price movement. Volatility spikes often signal either extreme fear or extreme euphoria.

Wealth Equation The universal law of compounding:

$$\text{Wealth} = (\text{Capital} \times \text{Accuracy} \times \text{Cycles Repeated})$$

Recommended Reading

The following books, papers, and resources deepen the principles covered in this book. They explore market cycles, psychology, valuation, risk management, and long-term thinking — the foundations of consistent Buy Low–Sell High execution.

1. Market Cycles & Behavioral Finance

"Mastering the Market Cycle" — Howard Marks A foundational book on how economic cycles, investor psychology, and valuation waves create opportunity.

"The Most Important Thing" — Howard Marks Short, powerful essays explaining risk, cycles, and second-level thinking.

"Thinking, Fast and Slow" — Daniel Kahneman The definitive guide to cognitive biases and emotional decision-making in financial markets.

"Misbehaving" — Richard Thaler A behavioral economics perspective on why markets move irrationally and how to benefit from it.

"Irrational Exuberance" — Robert Shiller A deep analysis of bubbles, manias, and how euphoria forms and collapses.

2. Valuation & Fundamental Analysis

"The Intelligent Investor" — Benjamin Graham The classic foundation of value investing: margin of safety, valuation, and emotional discipline.

"Security Analysis" — Graham & Dodd A comprehensive exploration of intrinsic value, financial statements, and valuation methods.

"One Up on Wall Street" — Peter Lynch Simple and practical lessons on recognizing undervalued opportunities in everyday businesses.

Investing: From Graham to Buffett and Beyond" — **Bruce Greenwald** A modern and practical approach to intrinsic valuation.

3. Psychology & Decision-Making

"Atomic Habits" — **James Clear** A practical guide to creating routines and systems — essential for consistent execution.

"The Psychology of Money" — **Morgan Housel** A short, powerful set of stories about behavior, risk, and long-term thinking.

"Deep Work" — **Cal Newport** Teaches focus, discipline, and system building — crucial for investors.

4. Risk Management & Long-Term Thinking

"Against the Gods" — **Peter Bernstein** A history of risk, probability, and uncertainty — with timeless lessons for investors.

"Fooled by Randomness" — **Nassim Nicholas Taleb** A powerful exploration of luck, noise, and survivorship bias in markets.

"The Black Swan" — **Nassim Nicholas Taleb** A must read on rare events, fragility, and protecting against catastrophic losses.

"Antifragile" — **Nassim Nicholas Taleb** A philosophy for benefiting from volatility and disorder — perfect for cycle-based investing.

5. Trend, Momentum, & Market Structure

"Trend Following" — **Michael Covel** A detailed study of how long-term trends form and why momentum works.

"Adaptive Markets" — **Andrew Lo** A synthesis of market evolution, psychology, and economic theory.

6. Optional: Crypto & New Asset Classes

Bitcoin Whitepaper — **Satoshi Nakamoto** The foundational paper that explains Bitcoin's technical and economic design.

"The Bitcoin Standard" — **Saifedean Ammous** A macro perspective on Bitcoin's long-term value framework.

These books deepen your understanding of cycles, behavior, valuation, and discipline — the same pillars behind the BL–SH System. Returning to them periodically will strengthen your judgment and improve your execution across every cycle.

www.ingramcontent.com/pod-product-compliance
Lightning Source LLC
Chambersburg PA
CBHW050525240926
51846CB00003B/700
* 9 7 8 9 3 5 5 2 5 8 4 6 5 *